To Jean from J.W.H.

D1386096

SEMINAR STUDIES IN HISTORY

Editor: Patrick Richardson

The Weimar Republic

SEMINAR STUDIES IN HISTORY

Editor: Patrick Richardson

A full list of titles in this
series will be found on the
back cover of this book

SEMINAR STUDIES IN HISTORY

The Weimar Republic

J.W.Hiden

Lecturer in European History,
University of Aberdeen

LONGMAN

Longman
1724-1974

LONGMAN GROUP LIMITED
London

Associated companies, branches and
representatives throughout the world

All rights reserved. No part of this publication
may be reproduced, stored in a retrieval system
or transmitted in any form or by any means —
electronic, mechanical, photocopying,
recording or otherwise — without the
prior permission of the copyright owner.

First published 1974

ISBN 0 582 35216 9

Printed in Great Britain by
Lowe & Brydone (Printers) Ltd., Thetford, Norfolk.

For Hugo

Contents

Acknowledgements

We are grateful to the following for permission to reproduce copyright material:

Allert de Lange N.V. and William Heinemann Ltd for an excerpt from *Through two decades* by T. Wolff; Bayer. Staatsministerium der Finanzen, Houghton Mifflin Company and Hutchinson Publishing Group Ltd for an excerpt from *Mein Kampf* translated by R. Mannheim; The Clarendon Press for excerpts from *The Reichswehr in Politics 1918–1933* by F. L. Carsten © 1966 Oxford University Press, reproduced by permission of The Clarendon Press, Oxford; Columbia University Press for an extract from *The Germans and their modern History* (1966) by Fritz Ernst; Dokumenten Verlag for excerpts from *Ursachen und Folgen* edited by H. Michaelis *et al*; Harald Boldt Verlag KG for an excerpt from *Akten der Reichskanzlei, Weimarer Republik, Das Kabinett Müller II* edited by Marin Vogt, Boldt Verlag, 5407 Boppard/Rhein, 1970; Libraire Armand Colin for 'Table of Election Results' from *L'Allemagne de Weimar* by G. Castellan edited by A. Colin; Translator and Wesleyan University Press for an excerpt from *Memoires* (1970) by H. Brüning translated by Claire Nix; Oxford University Press for excerpts from *The Speeches of Adolf Hitler,* April 1922–August 1939, translation edited by Norman H. Baynes published by Oxford University Press under the auspices of the Royal Institute of International Affairs; Oxford University Press, Inc. for an excerpt from *The German Inflation of 1923* by Fritz K. Ringer; Phaidon Press Limited and Praeger Publishers, Inc. for an excerpt from *The Political Institution of the German Revolution* by C. B. Burdick and R. H. Lutz and Rowohlt Verlag GmbH for an excerpt from *Der Fragebogen* by Ernst von Salomon, copyright 1951 by Rowohlt Verlag GmbH, Hamburg, English translation *The Answers,* Putnam, London 1954. The cover print is reproduced by courtesy of the Busch-Reisinger Museum, Harvard University.

Introduction to the Series

The seminar method of teaching is being used increasingly. It is a way of learning in smaller groups through discussion, designed both to get away from and to supplement the basic lecture techniques. To be successful, the members of a seminar must be informed — or else, in the unkind phrase of a cynic — it can be a 'pooling of ignorance'. The chapter in the textbook of English or European history by its nature cannot provide material in this depth, but at the same time the full academic work may be too long and perhaps too advanced.

For this reason we have invited practising teachers to contribute short studies on specialised aspects of British and European history with these special needs in mind. For this series the authors have been asked to provide, in addition to their basic analysis, a full selection of documentary material of all kinds and an up-to-date and comprehensive bibliography. Both these sections are referred to in the text, but it is hoped that they will prove to be valuable teaching and learning aids in themselves.

Note on the System of References:
A bold number in round brackets **(5)** in the text refers the reader to the corresponding entry in the Bibliography section at the end of the book.

A bold number in square brackets, preceded by 'doc' **[docs 6, 8]** refers the reader to the corresponding items in the section of Documents, which follows the main text.

PATRICK RICHARDSON
General Editor

Abbreviations

BVP   Bavarian People's Party (*Bayerische Volkspartei*)

DDP   German Democratic Party (*Deutsche Demokratische Partei*)

DVP   German People's Party (*Deutsche Volkspartei*)

DNVP   German National People's Party – Nationalists (*Deutsch-nationale Volkspartei*)

KPD   German Communist Party (*Kommunistische Partei Deutschlands*)

NSDAP   National Socialist German Workers' Party (*National-sozialistische Deutsche Arbeiterpartei*)

SPD   German Social Democratic Party (*Sozialdemokratische Partei Deutschlands*)

USPD   German Independent Social Democratic Party (*Unabhängige Sozialdemokratische Partei Deutschlands*)

PART ONE

Background

1 Constitution: after revolution

In the light of our present knowledge of the tragic end of the Weimar Republic it appears difficult to quarrel with Golo Mann's recent admonition on the subject of the Weimar Constitution. 'What is put down on paper at the beginning will influence future events without determining them' (25). A less cautious view of an English historian writing in 1926 reminds us, however, at least to make the effort to see how things looked before anyone had imagined the Nazi seizure of power. 'German democracy,' wrote Gooch, 'which was born in the trenches and inspired the revolution, found permanent expression in the Weimar Constitution' (16). In fact both authors, writing some forty years apart, saw the constitution as a framework which had to bear the weight of future developments, but Gooch's quotation more aptly stresses the point that the constitution itself was also the product of the past and that this process helped to determine what was put down on paper. To understand the framework of the Republic it follows that the Revolution must be understood, since it was the link between the former German Empire and the Weimar Republic.

If Gooch suggests that there were clearly 'democratic' trends in Germany before 1918, the wave of revolutionary disturbances which swept the country after the German Fleet's refusal to put to sea at Kiel on 28 October 1918 was less the product of political pressures than of war weariness, and this feeling was intensified by the sudden shock of Germany's imminent defeat after four years of brutal fighting (49). Through ignorance, impatience or scepticism, the German masses had no time for the ill-publicised constitutional reforms of October 1918. These went hand in hand with the effective loss of power by the military giants and wartime leaders Ludendorff and Hindenburg, and had transformed the Empire into a constitutional monarchy. The masses continued to regard the Kaiser as the reason for past troubles, the cause of their present suffering and the most important remaining obstacle to the signature of an armistice to end hostilities with the Allied Powers. In the face of such pressure existing order virtually collapsed. Yet the rapid spread throughout Germany of workers' and soldiers' councils on the model of those in the recent Russian revolution confirmed that the German masses also had political aims, if unspecified, that demanded more drastic changes **(45, 48)**. The Kaiser abdicated and power logically went to the party of the masses. In the first place then, the revolution was one which brought the German socialists to power. The Republic was proclaimed on 9 November 1918 and an all-socialist government was set up on 10 November. But what sort of socialists? The answer to this was to help determine the nature of the new Germany.

Conditions seemed to exist for a remodelling of society and a clean break with Wilhelmine Germany, but the German socialists were not prepared for revolution and were divided. The majority, made up of the Social Democratic Party (SPD) and led by Friedrich Ebert, continued to act and to think primarily in their prewar categories. In effect they had played down their revolutionary programme, first drawn up in Erfurt in 1891, and had accommodated themselves increasingly to existing conditions whilst working towards a more genuine constitutional monarchy **(29, 39, 86)**. This programme had been virtually fulfilled in October and the proclamation of the Republic ensured its completion. It was thus Ebert's intention to restore the conditions necessary to the holding of elections to a National Assembly. The larger body would then take the responsibility of drawing up a new constitution, though it is clear that the SPD leaders anticipated that, given the collapse of the old state, the elections would return the sort of socialist majorities which would make possible some restructuring of German society.

A minority of the original SPD had, however, broken away from the parent body in April 1917 to form the Independent German Social Democratic Party (USPD). The split was occasioned less by differences in ideology and more by differences between personalities and over tactics, in particular regarding the conduct of the war. The majority of the USPD leaders did not envisage the revolution developing along the lines of that which had brought the Bolsheviks to power in Russia in October 1917. On the other hand, leaders like Hugo Haase were realists enough to want a far more positive attitude taken towards the restructuring of German society, believing that opportunities should be grasped at once and a new order consolidated before the elections to a National Assembly, in order to forestall a regrouping of the powerful conservative forces of the old Empire, which would have minimised the effects of revolution **[doc. 1]**. They thus deplored the somewhat negative attitude of Ebert and his colleagues.

The hope that, faced with the problems of revolution, the socialist movement would regain its united strength, was seen in the mixed composition of the new government of 10 November 1918, the Council of Peoples' Commissars, with its three SPD and three USPD members. This derived its authority from the workers' and soldiers' councils. There remained the pressing problem of the third group of socialists known as the Spartacists, who had formed themselves on an antiwar basis round Karl Liebknecht in 1914, and included such inspired leaders as Rosa Luxemburg and Franz Mehring in their ranks. Although still attached to the USPD until they formed the German Communist Party (KPD) in December 1918, they propagated vigorously the idea of a seizure of power on the Russian model once the German revolution broke out. Together with the important group of radical shop stewards these formed a formidable pressure group for the new government to contend with. While not accepting the programme of the Spartacists the USPD leaders were extremely sensitive to the pull of the left and were also increasingly alienated from the SPD by Ebert's own over-zealous response to the exaggerated threat of communism. Such internal tensions were to make impossible the attainment of the dream of a united socialist movement, hammering out a new shape for German society and politics.

The SPD standpoint entailed by definition the suppression of extremist threats, and any such action was not betraying Ebert's view of the revolution as the moderate democratisation of the German state **(47)**. Nonetheless, Ebert's hasty acceptance of the offer of support to keep order and to crush bolshevism, which was made on behalf of the discredited officer corps of Wilhelmine Germany by Wilhelm Groener in his celebrated telephone call to Ebert on 10 November 1918 (see chapter 8), has been criticised in particular for the way in which it enabled the old army to carry over its power and traditions to the new Republic. It severely limited Ebert's freedom of manoeuvre, completely underestimating the threat from the right, and it aggravated the suspicions of the USPD about Ebert's easy relationships with the Wilhelmine bureaucracy in general, which continued to function throughout the revolution and seemed to provide further evidence of the SPD's indifference to radical changes in society. The meaning of the SPD's alliance with the army was seen in the bloody suppression of a Spartacist demonstration in Berlin on 6 December 1918 and the alienation of the USPD from the SPD was completed by their resignation from the government on 29 December 1918.

Ebert's policy, freed of the restraint of Haase and his colleagues, was taken to its logical conclusion when the SPD Minister of Defence,

Gustav Noske, availed himself of the services of the new *Freikorps* (volunteer) units. These had been formed under the old army officers and were used to crush the chaotic and ill-coordinated Spartacist 'rising' in January 1919. The murder of Liebknecht and Luxemburg on 15 January was a decisive enough answer to those few who wanted a Russian-style revolution in Germany **(49).** The brutal exercise was repeated by these forces, the basis of the new *Reichswehr* (see chapter 8), when they smashed the soviet that had held sway briefly in Munich in April **(102).** Ironically, Rosa Luxemburg had already admitted to herself the absence of any mass demand in Germany for a violent revolution **(103).** The mood of the masses was throughout antimilitary rather than anticapitalist, epitomised in the tearing off of officers' insignia on the one hand and the conciliatory agreements between the employers and workers of the Ruhr area on 18 November 1918 on the other **(49).** The great German Congress of Workers' and Soldiers' Deputies, held in Berlin between 16 and 19 December, endorsed Ebert's policy of preparing for elections to the National Assembly, thus rejecting revolution. Yet the demands were voiced for wider measures of socialisation and demilitarisation than Ebert appeared ready to consider, thus emphasising the failure of the SPD leaders to exploit fully the favourable opportunities to change German society and, again, giving substance to the accusations of the USPD.

The elections to the National Assembly were held on 19 January 1919 and they were, it is true, a victory for parliamentary democracy that would have been inconceivable before the revolution. On the other hand at a time when the harsh peace terms were not known and the mood of the times made Berlin too dangerous to house the Assembly which eventually met in Weimar (the city giving the Republic its name), voting did not bring the SPD the absolute majority necessary to implement even their programme. They were bound to rely on the support of the other two parties who were to form with them the so-called 'Weimar coalition', namely the Centre Party and the Democrats. The very appearance of these non-socialist parties, let alone the political organisations representing the powerful reactionary forces of prewar Germany, indicated the renewed confidence of those influential sectors of German society that had been initially so overwhelmed by the revolution. The new Republic would thus have to rest on a compromise between the very forces that had been in conflict in the German Empire. It was, moreover, a compromise which had been made possible in the last resort by the use of force. Yet, arguably, continuity was natural; the balance of forces had at least been weighted by revolution in favour of the democratic mood that Gooch observed, and the theoretically workable compromise was enshrined in the constitution duly passed by the National Assembly after much debate on 31 July 1919.

Early drafts of the Constitution were ready not much more than a month after the outbreak of revolution, but the views of its chief author, the Democrat Hugo Preuss, were modified both by the arguments of the parties in the National Assembly through the twenty-eight member all-party committee chaired by another Democrat, Conrad Haussmann, and by the representations of the various German states through the Committee of States that was set up on 25 January 1919. The responsible and meticulous discussion carried on in these groups and in the full Assembly ensured that the constitution, if a compromise, was hardly a hasty one. The text reaffirmed in Article 1 that power derived from the people and that the state was a democracy and a republic. The German parliament (*Reichstag*) was where sovereignty resided, and it was to be elected every four years. In the postwar and post-revolutionary atmosphere the urge to extend the vote to men and women of twenty-one years of age was irresistible, even if this enfranchised politically uneducated and frankly hostile masses. The system of representation was proportional, whereby a party organisation drew up a list for which people voted rather than for a specific local candidate and each party was allowed one representative for every 60,000 votes cast in its favour. This did nothing to discourage the formation of smaller parties which, if they never attracted much support (28), certainly confused issues in later years (89).

The functions of the Reichstag cannot be discussed without reference to the creation of the post of Reich President. Notwithstanding the doubts of the SPD, the other parties wanted the President to be able to act as a counterweight to the Reichstag, and thus he was to be elected by a separate popular vote every seven years, although this provision did not apply in the case of Friedrich Ebert when he became the Republic's first President in August 1919. The controversial Article 48 of the constitution gave the President special powers to use in an emergency but the Reichstag could reject any measures he proposed. Moreover, the President's actions needed the counter-signature of the Reich Chancellor, whom admittedly the President appointed but who was responsible with his cabinet to the Reichstag and whom the President had to dismiss on any vote of no confidence by the Reichstag. In view of the fateful use of the presidential powers during the crisis that brought Hitler to power it is well to point out and to stress that there was never an attempt at a presidential coup d'état in Weimar Germany. The emergency powers of the President could on the other hand be of use in difficult periods, for example in

7

1923 **(29)**. How much weight should be attached to the contention that the use of such emergency powers positively encouraged the tendency of political parties to shun unpleasant duties is still a matter for argument. Certainly many Germans appeared to see the President as a sort of emperor-substitute and in regarding his office as a guarantee against parliamentary absolutism betrayed their own cynicism about democratic government. Yet the key would appear to lie also with the personality of the President, and one recent German study of Ebert is convincing in its demonstration that his reluctance to interfere actively in important political matters went to the point of weakening his office. This is a reminder, useful even at this stage, that a number of complicated factors interacting with each other affected the outcome of the crisis in Germany after 1929; the President's rôle will be considered again in due course.

The differing views on authority within the new Republic were bound to affect also the complicated balance of power between central and local government **(17)**, as can be seen from an examination of the second chamber set up by the constitution, the *Reichsrat*. Like its predecessor under the Bismarckian constitution, the *Bundesrat* (Federal Council), the new Reichsrat reflected the need of Weimar governments to come to terms with the long and powerful tradition of separatism in Germany. The different German states strongly and successfully defended themselves against Preuss' original plans to readjust their boundaries, except for the special case of Thuringia **(51)**, although their continued federal association with the new Reich was no longer based, as it had once been after 1871, on their existence as sovereign states. Their designation under the new constitution as *Länder* (Land— province) signified a demotion from sovereign independence and thus considerably curtailed the powers of the Reichsrat. This continued to represent the governments of the different states but was essentially, again unlike the former Bundesrat, subservient to the Reichstag. Its most important power, that of vetoing the Reichstag's acts, could be overridden by a two-thirds vote of the lower chamber. The attempt was made to ensure that Prussia did not dominate the Reichsrat as it had once dominated the Bundesrat **(13)** by providing that no Land should be allowed more than two-fifths of the votes in the chamber and by permitting only half the Prussian votes to go to the Prussian government whilst the ·remainder were distributed among the Prussian provinces.

The Reich government thus had considerable powers and its laws took precedence over those of the various state governments. The constitution completed the control of the Reich government over foreign affairs, the armed forces (in theory; see chapter 8) and communications, and of particular importance was the control by the central government of the machinery of taxation after Matthias Erzberger became Minister of Finance in June 1919 (10). Yet the greater powers of direct legislation given to the Reich were offset to a certain extent by considerable powers remaining with the different Länder, notably in the sphere of police (24), judiciary and education. Regrettably there was no guarantee that a Land might not deliberately obstruct central government policies, particularly in the case of Bavaria where there was less respect for the Republic (29). The fact that Prussia still carried enormous weight helped partially to compensate for this since it now became a stronghold of the Social Democrats (13).

In discussing the constitution we have passed gradually from talk about revolution to a survey of some of the more traditional problems of Germany that preoccupied the National Assembly. It would be reasonable to call the finished text a synthesis between progressive political and social ideas and the desire to protect traditional institutions, and the second part of the constitution, elaborating the fundamental rights of German democracy, epitomised the scrupulous effort to be fair. Historians have, however, come to dwell precisely on the continuity and on the way in which older parties reappeared; on the way in which the army retained its position; on the way in which the old bureaucracy of the German Empire continued to function; on the way in which the various councils for economic control could hardly lead to socialisation now that the socialists relied on other parties to support them. The constitution satisfied no one party entirely, but it was accepted by 262 to 75 votes, being opposed outright by only the German Nationalists and the German People's Party. If Ebert and his colleagues signally failed to make the most of their chances they had thus apparently provided what most people found acceptable after the Great War. Nothing would ever be the same; the traditional forces did have to operate within a totally new political framework and this the constitution provided. Legislation was only the beginning, and no matter what was 'put down on paper' much depended on the problems the Republic had to face.

2 Versailles, truth and fiction

If the constitution may be regarded as the framework for the internal developments of the Weimar Republic, it would seem self-evident to see the Versailles treaty as the framework in which the country's external relations had to develop. A point of fundamental importance, however, is that the terms of the treaty signed between Germany and the Allied and Associated Powers at Versailles were so objectionable to the German masses that how to react to those terms, and thus how to conduct foreign policy, formed the subject of prolonged dispute between parties and was therefore directly related to the internal peace of the Republic. The impact of the peace terms when they became officially known to Germans in a draft form on 7 May 1919 was such that it led to the resignation of the Republic's first parliamentary government under Philipp Scheidemann, and a refusal to sign the terms. Yet Scheidemann's government was based on the coalition of political forces that had captured three-quarters of the votes in the elections to the National Assembly, that between the SPD, the Democrats and the Centre Party, the so-called 'Weimar coalition'. Only when it became quite clear, even to the most important military leaders, that there was no question of resisting the Allied threat to use force, did a new SPD-Centrist coalition under the Social Democrat Gustav Bauer take the responsibility of signing the treaty on 28 June 1919. The 138 votes in the National Assembly against authorising the government to sign (after the debate of 22 and 23 June) which included the Democrats and predictably the Nationalists, were only the most immediately obvious sign of rejection and resentment felt by the entire German population. So much so that Ebert's election by popular vote, as was mentioned, had to be foregone in order to prevent the possible choice of a candidate from the right.

The disparity between the general reaction against the Treaty in Germany and the way in which Weimar governments went on to adapt to those terms as far as possible after 1919 remains one of the most interesting features of the Republic's history. More than anything, the addition of the words 'truth and fiction' to this section's title reflects the reaction of the German public. This was determined by certain fundamental if mistaken beliefs, not the least important being that Germany had fought the war for defensive purposes to avoid the threat of 'encirclement' by the other powers before 1914. Secondly, that the peace would be a 'just' peace, based on the celebrated Fourteen Points made by the American President Wilson in January 1918, which had been accepted in principle during the pre-Armistice negotiations in early November 1918 (76). Thirdly, that the proclamation of a Republic, with new forms of government and professedly new democratic values, made it even more necessary that the new Germany should not be treated in a punitive fashion.

It is still almost invariably the accepted approach of general accounts of the Republic to stress the failure of the Scheidemann government to prepare the German public for the disappointment which German government officials well knew was in store (28). These after all had seen at close hand in the preliminary stages of the armistice negotiations that the grim mood of the Allies, themselves subject to severe domestic pressures to negotiate a harsh peace, did not promise an especially favourable interpretation of any of the points at issue. This pessimistic assumption was supported by the Allied decision not to invite the Germans to participate in the drafting of the peace treaty and thus to save time and to preserve their own unity of approach as far as possible (76, 82). Yet precisely these factors helped to determine the German government's own tactics, namely to press in any way possible for a favourable interpretation on all points and this guided the work of the enormous body of officials in the special section set up in the German Foreign Office who proceeded to prepare a battery of written pleas and arguments for the attention of the Paris Peace Conference. In short, German revisionism dates less from the presentation of the actual treaty, as is implied in many of the existing descriptions of the shock impact of the draft peace terms, than from the moment the Germans laid down their arms.

If one visualises a more or less continuous government line running from November 1918 onwards, then it is easier to see that for the German government to have prepared its own public in the way suggested would have been to minimise the effectiveness of its 'battle of the notes'. The enforced signature of the treaty confirmed the worst of existing fears and confirmed the need for a more long-term and cautious running campaign to modify the treaty terms. Firm rejection of the treaty was also part of the revisionist tactics and if the importance of precedent and wording in international agreements is admitted it is also possible to see more than senseless protests in the excessive concern of the German government to refute the notion of war guilt expressed in Article 231 of the treaty [**doc. 5**]. That this whole process entailed the sort of gap we have observed between government and public awareness of the implications of the treaty was an unfortunate corollary of official tactics but it was not impossible to imagine the gap closing somewhat in due course since the peace terms still had to be executed and, because this required the co-operation of German officialdom, there was the hope of future bargaining.

This might not be immediately appreciated by summarising the main terms as they stood on paper in 1919. The economic provisions of the treaty were of course a severe shock, given the postwar distress of Germany, as Keynes argued almost too brilliantly in his famous book *The Economic Consequences of the Peace* (**97**). The impact of the reparations that were legally justified by the 'war-guilt' clause 231, is discussed in chapter 5, but other parts of the treaty appeared equally severe since Germany's overseas investment and property in enemy countries were confiscated, arguably more damaging than the enforced loss of her colonies. The ability of Germany to promote her economic recovery through the resumption of her prewar foreign trading was threatened by the compulsion to give the Allied powers most favoured nation treatment and this, with the five year ban on protective tariffs, affected the terms of any German trade treaties. The loss of resources in the detached territories of the East and of the coal in the Saar region must be placed on the debit side (chapter 5). A reasoned rehearsal of the now familiar arguments for and against these terms is superfluous here, especially since German opinion did not care for such reasoning, but it is worth stressing firstly, that much depended on the future development of Germany's economy and the outcome of the reparations issue; secondly, that Germany's economic weight in East Europe was to remain considerable, an enormously important factor if one recalls the attention focused by the whole of Europe on exploiting the gigantic Russian markets.

The territorial settlement at Versailles arguably caused greater public resentment in Germany than reparations. In the West, Alsace-Lorraine was restored to France. Allied forces were to occupy the left bank of the Rhine for fifteen years, the withdrawal to take place in three stages of five years, possibly earlier if Germany fulfilled her treaty obligations and behaved. The left bank of the Rhine and the thirty-mile-wide strip on the right bank were permanently demilitarised. The Saar was to be administered by the League for fifteen years, after which a plebiscite would determine its fate. Frontier adjustments were also made in favour of Belgium in Eupen, Malmedy and Moresnet, and in Denmark's favour, after a plebiscite, in North Schleswig. On the eastern frontiers of Germany the fulfilment of number 13 of Wilson's Fourteen Points meant a corridor between East Prussia and the rest of the Reich to ensure that the new Polish state had 'secure access to the sea' via Danzig. Thus the provinces of Posen and West Prussia were lost to Poland. Plebiscites in 1920 and 1921 left Germany in control of the disputed frontier districts of Marienwerder and Allenstein as well as nearly two-thirds of the vital territory of Upper Silesia. If a million Germans thus fell to Polish rule, these were surrounded by areas predominantly settled by Poles. Moreover, the Poles were not given the city of Danzig outright, but its German character was in effect recognised by making it a free city under the supervision of a High Commissioner appointed by the League of Nations with Poland supervising the city's foreign relations (68). Less violently contested in Germany until after 1933 was the fate of the Germans left in the areas ceded to Czechoslovakia, as was true of the loss of the German Baltic port at Memel to Lithuania, whose support the German government desired against Poland. In spite of German propaganda, it could be argued that the only outright violation of Wilson's professed ideal of self-determination over the German territorial settlement was the refusal of the Allies to permit the joining together of Austria and Germany (17, 53).

Again, the arguments for and against this territorial settlement have often been given at prodigious length, but they hardly impressed the German masses, who were incensed in particular by the shock of being forced to treat the long-dominated and partitioned Poland as a great power [doc. 15]. Revision of the eastern frontiers was bound to be a constant tenet of all Weimar governments and political parties, and if success in this direction seemed far away in 1919, certain factors were already working in Germany's favour and were to help her foreign policy. In the first place, the original French demands, which had included the annexation of the whole of the Rhineland and a far more generous treatment of the Poles, had been modified because of Anglo-American pressures. Such moderation seemed in order to those politicians who feared driving Germany into a dangerously revisionist mood and who in some degree felt that Germany should be sound enough to resist the apparent, if vastly overestimated, threat of communist infiltration of Central Europe (75). The second point is that in 1920 the Anglo-American guarantee of the Rhineland settlement lapsed owing to the American Senate's refusal to ratify the Versailles Treaty, and France therefore logically sought to tie together still more closely the territorial settlement on the West and East of Germany by entering into close treaty arrangements with the states that had formerly been part of the Russian empire, in particular with Poland. Yet France depended in the long run on British support, and it was precisely in East Europe that British commitments to the new *status quo* were most suspect **(76, 77)**, and where German economic influence, which in itself brought political power, was so difficult to counter. This was particularly true since the Peace Conference could find no answer as yet to the problem of what to do about Russia, and this left room for German governments to move **[docs. 6, 15]**. Fear ensured that France, with her inferior population growth, would press for strict interpretations of the Versailles terms, but she could not do it alone as was shown in 1923, in spite of the weakness of the German military machine as a result of the military clauses of Versailles (see chapter 8).

Although Germany lost some 13 per cent of her territory and some 6 million subjects, it is no longer acceptable to blame the ultimate failure of the Republic on the Treaty of Versailles, and even its economic effects are disputed, given the economic 'recovery' of Germany in the middle-twenties (chapter 5). For Weimar governments there was a real possibility to work patiently and skilfully in their relations with the foreign powers and to 'undertake the unavoidable in such a way as to derive the greatest possible credit for doing so, both from . . . antagonists and other interested parties' **(55)**. Yet there remained the perennial problem for Weimar governments of convincing internal opposition of the validity of this approach **[doc. 11]** since the German public continued to resent the violation of the fundamental beliefs mentioned at the beginning of this discussion. Germany's exclusion from the new peace-keeping organisation, the League of Nations, underlined the arguments of German nationalists against the *Diktat* of Versailles. This disillusionment made it easier for Germans to accept the false notion propagated by rightist and nationalist circles that such an 'unjust' peace need never have been signed in the first place **[doc. 10]**. To accept this one had to believe, incredibly enough and in spite of the mass revulsion against war which nurtured the revolution, that Germany had not been militarily defeated but could have fought on had the army not been 'stabbed in the back' by the civilian leaders. This argument led to a concentration of nationalist resentment not on the foreign powers who had fought against Germany but on the original 'November criminals', who had initiated the armistice talks and, by implication, on any politicians or groups who believed in the efficacy of slow but sure revisionism by way of working with the former enemy powers. The pernicious effects of the Versailles treaty lie thus in the way it created added dimensions to existing internal conflicts and contradictions which had, to some extent, survived the revolution **(29)**. Perhaps the only clear way to demonstrate this is to examine some of the fundamental problems of the Weimar Republic before turning to the final crisis to see how the complex interaction of numerous factors brought Hitler to power.

PART TWO

Problems

3 Coalitions and party politics

The limited nature of the changes wrought by the revolution was emphasised by the confident reappearance in the National Assembly of the prewar political parties. The number of these ensured that henceforth all German governments would have to be based on a group of parties and that efficient government entailed co-operation between any parties that made up a given coalition. In effect this meant the survival into the Republic of the unresolved structural crisis of Wilhelmine Germany and social conflicts were renewed in the parliaments of the new Republic. This intrinsic weakness predisposed German party politics towards selfish battles of interests which were likely in turn to exaggerate the severity of any internal or external crisis facing the Republic, but it is useful to emphasise the changed context in which interparty disputes were renewed. The location of sovereignty in the Reichstag meant at least that party conflicts could be continued to government level, and if this process made for hesitant and fitful policies the painful struggle was, given the lack of experience, perhaps unavoidable if any political stability and tradition were to emerge. This section concerns itself therefore chiefly with those parties which were, at least in principle, prepared to try to evolve and to adapt themselves to new responsibilities and which were responsible, by and large, for the constructive policies of the Republic, the Centre Party, the SPD, the *Deutsche Demokratische Partei* (Democrats, DDP) and the *Deutsche Volkspartei* (German People's Party, DVP).

The four parties shared, or came to share for a period, a commitment to preserve the Republic, self-evident in the case of the SPD and very clearly expressed by the DDP, which was founded on 25 November 1918 from the old Progressive Party and the left wing of the National Liberals (89, 90) and sought to rally the bourgeois liberal, intellectual forces of Wilhelmine Germany to the new order [doc. 3]. The *Zentrumspartei* or Centre Party, founded in 1870, was hostile to the revolution and at first not positively in favour of the Republic, but it had at least shared with the SPD a longstanding interest in defending parliamentary institutions in Wilhelmine Germany, and its extremely varied social composition predisposed it towards compromise within the new Republic, especially since its left wing had been strengthened under Matthias Erzberger as a result of the war **(88, 89)**. Its support of centralised government in Germany brought it into sharp conflict with the other major Catholic party, the Bavarian People's Party **(BVP)**, but the two parties invariably combined over the all important defence of the Catholic church, culture and educational matters. The DVP, on the other hand, was a rightist party founded by Gustav Stresemann and Hugo Stinnes from the right wing of the old National Liberals in late November 1918. Initially hostile to the Republic, monarchist and anti-socialist, the influence of Stresemann in particular swung the DVP towards responsible work in the Republic after the excesses of 1919–22 and the economic collapse of 1923 **(91)**.

The period 1919–23, which saw rightist and leftist risings, and political assassinations, as well as a frightening economic collapse, was bound to be an acutely testing time for the new style of coalition governments since they were faced with countless unpopular decisions. Postwar discontent manifested itself in the well-known swing towards political extremes. Whereas, for example, the 'Weimar coalition' of SPD-Centre-DDP had been supported by three-quarters of the electorate in the elections to the National Assembly, it was supported by only a minority of voters in the elections to the first Reichstag in June 1920 [doc. 4]. To get an immediate idea of the alarming difficulties in the way of formulating and executing consistent policies it might be noted that these four parties were variously involved in no less than nine governments between February 1919 and the end of 1923. Such facts do indeed justify the assertions of historians that only after 1923 and before 1929 is it possible to speak of parliamentary government in any meaningful sense **(29)**, particularly in view of the extensive use that was made of Article 48 between 1919 and 1923 in order to push through vital legislation. As against this bleak view it has been pointed out that in these years at least Article 48 was a stabilising factor and that out of the turmoil came quite positive achievements, not the least being economic reconstruction and a definitive step along the road to resolving Germany's external problems (chapters 4 and 5).

Moreover, the constant struggle against extremism provided invaluable experience to the coalition parties since the sense of crisis strengthened the hands of all politicians who were struggling to make the most of what chances there were for constructive action, as could be seen in the climactic formation of the 'Grand Coalition' during the crisis of 1923, when Stresemann's first cabinet was based on the SPD, DDP, Centre and his own DVP. It remains true, however, that for all the 'first uneasy groping for their new role' **(89)**, the four parties in question could not paper over essential differences and that these, paradoxically, became more pronounced with the passing of crisis and the more indulgent mood engendered by the stability of the years 1924 to 1928.

This is not to say that parliamentary experience did not continue to grow in the relatively stable period between the economic crisis of 1923 and that of 1929, but success in this direction was qualified by the ultimate failure of the respective parties to strike a proper balance between the economic and social interests which they represented and the interests of the state [doc. 17]. Perhaps this simply showed once again that it took time and much trial and error for the parties to discard the bad habits and practices of Wilhelmine Germany and to grow into the responsibilities of their new roles, but the absence of more positive and forceful leadership in the major parties made matters worse. In particular this charge has rightly been levelled at the SPD leaders whose original failure to exploit their power during the revolution developed into a process of 'continuous error' **(39)**. They failed to make of their early association with the bourgeois parties, or so-called 'democratic middle' of DDP, Centre and DVP, a lasting and constructive partnership, although they had jettisoned their left wing and, in view of their acceptance of the Versailles treaty, could hardly hope for the support of the nationalist right. At the end of 1923 the SPD opted out of direct governmental responsibility, reverting to its 'habit of opposition', and did not re-enter the government until 1928.

Admittedly the SPD leadership had its difficulties, particularly its dependence on the trade union movement **(2, 90)** which limited its freedom of choice somewhat; admittedly the effort had to be made in the face of economic distress not to lose votes to the German communists (KPD), who appealed to the militant, young and unemployed working class sectors. The reunification of USPD and SPD in 1922 testified to the growing concern of the socialist movement to protect the interests of its class. Yet the decision to leave the bourgeois coalitions was the result of misguided tactics, and it can be convincingly argued that a better if more difficult way to protect interests and to counter the appeal of the KPD would have been to continue trying to evolve attractive and constructive compromise politics from inside the government. In opposition the SPD continued to give important support to Republican ideals and, if it chimed with their view of things, to the governments in office, but this was hardly the best way to exploit the impressive mass basis of the party which remained until 1932 the largest in the Reichstag.

These developments were bound to affect in turn the internal condition of the three parties which, minus the SPD, formed five out of the seven administrations between 1924 and the end of June 1928 (the other two governments including the German National People's Party, DNVP). Both the Centre Party and the DDP had an inbuilt distrust of socialist policies, less those that aimed at improvement of the working class than those which appeared to threaten private property, and this of course applied with greater force to the DVP which was in effect 'the parliamentary mouthpiece of industry' **(29, 91)**. The tendency of both Centrist and DVP leaders towards co-operation with the rightist DNVP was thus more pronounced after 1923. Stresemann was under great pressure from the right wing of his DVP to reconsider his tactics at the end of 1923. During that year the transformation of Stresemann, the wartime annexationist, to responsible party leader was completed. His growing determination to bring stability to Germany was reflected in his effort to keep together the 'Grand Coalition' on which he based his government after becoming Chancellor in August 1923. His success in bringing his party to accept the burden, with the Centre, DDP and SPD, of ending passive resistance in the Ruhr was remarkable, and he desperately wanted the middle of the road policies to continue in the interests of Germany's very existence. 'I regard it as my duty, as a party man and minister, to do all I can to unite the German people for these decisions, and not to force upon them the question: bourgeois or socialist' **(91)**. The SPD defection was therefore certain to intensify Stresemann's problems. To make matters worse the elections of 4 May 1924 showed how little appeal to voters had the courageous achievement of stabilisation and currency reform (chapter 5). The DVP, DDP and SPD all lost ground whereas the DNVP appeared to reap the rewards of opposition to unpopular policies by becoming the second largest party in the Reichstag **[doc. 4]**. This reinforced the determination of Stresemann's critics in the DVP to involve the nationalists in the responsibilities of government and thus to get their support as well as taking the sting out of the violence of rightist opposition to the Republic and its policies. There appeared to be some hope for this after 1923, the attitude of the DNVP between 1919 and 1923 notwithstanding **(117)** (chapter 7). For any coalition to govern effectively after 1923 concessions had to be made for support from left or right or both, or, given the SPD decision to remain in opposition, to include the nationalists in the government, which is what happened under Chancellor Luther in 1925 and Chancellor Marx in 1927.

As suggested, such conditions hardly encouraged the subjugation of party interests to those of the state, but there were tantalising vistas of better things. Perhaps not surprisingly, Stresemann had something to do with this. After his chancellorship ended he remained foreign minister for the next six years, and his work in this office helped to bring some coherence to the political forces represented in the Reichstag. By and large the SPD and trade unions, as well as the moderate bourgeois parties, the DDP and Centre, supported his foreign policy. True, Stresemann's foreign policy never gained the total support of his own party, let alone the DNVP, but by insisting on the 'primacy' of foreign affairs Stresemann hoped that in time his diplomatic successes and his active trade policy would influence the nationalists towards a more reasonable attitude and thus benefit domestic affairs. The DNVP was after all split over the Dawes plan, with its important economic pressure groups (chapter 7) in favour of it, and the DNVP were persuaded to remain in the government long enough for the Locarno treaties to be negotiated. Their renewed and bitter campaigns against the Locarno policies thereafter could not, whilst Stresemann was in office and whilst his policies continued to be successful at an international level, bring them any real benefits [doc. 7].

It was, of course, significantly less easy for the middle parties to evolve consistent policies in domestic affairs and thus to counter the incessant propaganda from right and left. Trade unions for example (even the Christian trade unions that were affiliated to the 'loyal' Centre Party) and the SPD were in a position to resist legislation over wages or working hours whilst these matters were dear to the heart of the DVP. The DVP's interest, on the other hand, in developing maximum exports appeared to be at odds with the pressure coming from the 'agrarian' sectors of the DNVP (chapter 7) for protective tariffs to counter the attraction of cheap agricultural imports, which was also obviously opposed by working class interests. In short, whilst there was some possibility of compromise between the middle parties and the two 'wings', the DNVP and SPD, co-operation rarely went beyond tactical alliances made for specific purposes. It had 'little permanence in view of the deep ideological and socio-economic rifts which class conflict, accentuated by the reparations question and the distribution of its financial burdens, produced in the Reichstag' (29). The 'zig-zag' course of policy making which this state of affairs entailed did indeed do much to discredit the notion of parliamentary government among the German public at large, disillusioned as it was by the rigidity of party organisations and principles and disparaging about the 'horse-trading' which accompanied the formation of each new coalition government (2, 11). The evolution of cabinet traditions was virtually non-existent since ministers were too much at the mercy of interparty disputes and of their parliamentary factions. Thus the development of a proper working relationship between government and legislative body remained fitful, as was shown by the occasional resort to the device of a cabinet of above party 'experts' or 'personalities' (chapter 9). This certainly made it easier for sceptics to see promise only in the President's powers and in the day-to-day continuity of the work of the bureaucracy. That party leaders themselves were only too well aware of this can be seen in the plans for reform which were put forward at various times to define more suitably the role which parties should play in the governmental process (29), a subject on which the constitution had been merely vague.

Of interest, however, to the historian looking for the might-have-beens of the Republic is that the easy ridicule of the parliamentary process by the extremist parties as well as the press organs obscured the elements of promise, already briefly mentioned, which a more dis-passionate observer of the scene could have found. It detracted from the constant and unfailing effort of German Social Democracy to keep alive the values of the Republic; it minimised the importance of the continuous presence and effort in the coalitions of the DVP and Centre Party, which helped to compensate for the continuing decline of German liberalism – marked in the original split between DVP and DDP in 1918 and in the continuing election losses of the DDP thereafter. It minimised the importance of the Centre Party's sincere efforts to go beyond a strictly confessional basis and to bridge party differences by attempting to work with the DNVP at a national level and the Social Democrats in the largest state, Prussia (2, 90). Such important elements of rapprochement should not be pushed aside by hindsight. These impulses did something to counteract the historic tendency of German parties since 1848 to splinter into factional interest; a tendency taken to absurdity in the growth of even smaller, powerless yet confusing parties (like the German Business Party) from 1 per cent in 1919 to 8 per cent in 1930 (89). The process of rapprochement must also be seen in the light of extremist efforts on the right and left to discredit the Republican institutions. Thus, if it is indeed permissible to see in the behaviour of political leaders and parties after 1929 the outcome of earlier flaws and errors, it is also vital to stress the quite extraordinary nature of the years between 1929 and 1933.

4 Foreign Policy

For most Germans foreign policy meant a continuous and unremitting effort to revise the terms of the Treaty of Versailles, but if the end was agreed the means were not, and the conduct of foreign relations played its part in intensifying party political disputes. Admittedly, all shades of political opinion saw some virtue during the early years 1919–23 in being obstructive about the execution of the terms which officially came into force on 10 January 1920 – thus the effective avoidance of the clauses demanding action against the Kaiser and war criminals and the defiant German propaganda to disprove the charges of war guilt, the temporising of German governments over the demands to dismantle the paramilitary organisations and the outright hostility shown towards the various Allied control commissions watching over the implementation of the peace terms.

Yet the mood of resistance was matched by the greater determination of the Allies, and of France in particular, to end German prevarications. On 5 May 1921 the Allied London Ultimatum called firmly for the proper execution of the treaty terms and in particular for the acceptance by Germany of the new schedule for reparations payments (chapter 5). Since three Rhine ports had already been occupied by the Allies on 8 M..rch 1921, the point was taken, none the less courageously, by the new Chancellor from the Centre Party, Joseph Wirth, who in his two administrations between 10 May 1921 and late November 1922, developed the policy of 'fulfilment'. This was a necessary expedient based on the premise that to show determined good faith in trying to carry out the peace terms properly would not only demonstrate how impossible a task this was, but would therefore also induce the Allied powers to be more lenient in interpreting the treaty. Such a policy was supported in general by the 'Weimar coalition' but was bitterly opposed by the nationalists [doc. 11]. The violence of the mood engendered by the latter's reactions expressing itself in the murder in August 1921 of Matthias Erzberger (the German representative on the armistice commission in November 1918). The success of any

attempt to counteract the appeal of nationalist criticism was thus
bound to depend in part on rapid results from the policy of fulfilment.
Yet the intractable nature of the reparations problems precluded such
results, and after Wirth's resignation in November 1922, the 'business
ministry' of Dr Wilhelm Cuno was left to face French action in the Ruhr
in 1923, making the German Nationalists only too happy with the
policy of 'passive resistance' against the Allies (chapter 5).

Wirth, however, cannot be judged without looking at his government's contribution to the development of Germany's relations with
Soviet Russia. Much attention has been lavished on the 'Unholy
Alliance' (59) of defeated Germany and a Russia that was ostracised by
the West's aversion to Bolshevism. In fact co-operation between the
two 'outcasts' rested firmly on a basis of mutual self-interest and was
never an 'alliance' in any formal sense. Firstly, the German demand for
new markets was matched by the desperate need of the weakened
Soviet state for foreign aid and capital investment. Secondly, the vast
spaces of Russia, inaccessible to Allied control commissions, offered
hope for Germany's future secret development of military weapons and
techniques (138, 141, 144). Thirdly, the prospects were excellent for a
revival of the traditional German-Russian co-operation against the Polish
state. Russia had lost territories to Poland by the Treaty of Riga in
March 1921, and both Russia and Germany were additionally hostile to
the fact that in the French system of alliances Poland was to play a
central role in forming a 'barrier' of states between them (72, 61, 62)
[doc. 15]. In short, Soviet Russia could apparently hasten Germany's
return to great power status by helping to develop Germany's economic
and military potential. Moreover, since the Russians were not bound by
any peace treaty with the Allies, they could theoretically initiate diplomatic moves in Germany's interests but for the moment outside
Germany's power, which became for example a very real possibility
when the Red armies almost defeated Poland in 1920 (72, 138)
[doc. 6]. So striking were these prospects to key economic thinkers, to
military leaders like Seeckt (chapter 8), and to men like Baron Ago von
Maltzan, head of the Russian department of the German Foreign Office,
that they believed Germany's foreign policy orientation should be not
to the West but to the East, to Russia. Seeckt authorised preliminary
contacts with the Russians with a view to military collaboration after
his meeting with Karl Radek, Lenin's agent in Berlin, in early January
1920. In 1920 too, unofficial German-Russian economic contacts at
private level steadily increased. The resumption of normal German-
Soviet relations, which would entail recognition of Soviet Russia, was,
however, a political step of the first importance and would have angered

the Allied powers (31, 59).

The attitude of the German political leaders was therefore more cautious, and under foreign ministers like Adolf Köster in 1920 and Walther Simons in the early part of 1921 German-Russian relations were not permitted to develop too quickly. Typically, the German-Soviet provisional commercial agreement of 6 May 1921, though far more important, was not signed until the British government had taken a similar step (59). The policy of fulfilment launched by Wirth would have been less credible had it been accompanied by obviously closer ties with Russia, but the fact remains that not only was Wirth in favour of a more active Russian policy, in part because of his own dislike of Poland, but that in 1921 conditions favoured such a policy. The introduction in Russia of the New Economic Policy of Lenin, which favoured the limited return of some private enterprise, provided the suitable environment for German investment there. Furthermore, in the calculations of the Reparations commission (see chapter 5) there had been room left for Russia to exercise the right that was theoretically due to her according to Article 116 of Versailles to claim war damages against Germany. If this seemed unlikely in view of Lenin's attack on the 'robber peace' of Versailles, the situation could be changed in the event of closer relations between Russia and the Allies, and it was therefore in Wirth's interest not to let the policy of fulfilment lead to a worsening of German-Russian relations (87). Unlike Seeckt [doc. 15], for example, the political leaders kept open both options, East and West. Pressure on Wirth to commit himself more to the Russian connection intensified, firstly as the outcome of the plebiscite over Silesia in 1921 further inflamed German opinion against the Poles and secondly as the reparations crisis developed. On forming his second administration, Wirth encouraged the more active phase of the secret German-Russian exchanges which, after stops and starts, produced the eventual text of the Rapallo agreement between Germany and Russia, signed on 16 April 1922 during the World Economic Conference at Genoa (87). A study of this treaty's implications throws light generally on Weimar diplomacy.

In the first place, although a German historian recently stressed the aggressive nature of the Rapallo policy, the agreement was signed only after it had become fairly clear that, given especially the 'hard line' towards Germany of the new French leader Poincaré, Germany could expect few concessions at the Genoa Conference over the Versailles terms, in particular those relating to reparations. Even the German foreign minister, Walther Rathenau, whose name had been associated with fulfilment and who valued close work with the Allied pow' recognised this (71, 87). In the second place, the Russians had in effect made it clear that they did not accept the premises on which the Genoa conference was held, the first postwar conference to include the Russians. Lloyd George's dream of a restored European economy had included the plan for a world consortium at Genoa to exploit Russian trade. The Russians preferred the politically safer road of concentrating on the economic aid of individual countries, especially that of Germany and were not above playing on German fears about Article 116 to achieve their end. The Rapallo agreement thus shattered the conference and confirmed the worst fears of the French about German-Russian retaliation against Versailles.

Yet, arguably, the French would have continued to take a hard line towards Germany in any event and the Rapallo agreement did not in the least mean that German foreign policy would now be chiefly concerned with Russia. Admittedly it put the Poles under greater pressure by emphasising their dangerous position, and historians seem to be agreed that the pact marked the beginning of a greater freedom of movement for German policy-makers, giving them a useful lever in their dealings with the Allied powers. Yet these were more psychological advantages, not to be found in the text of the agreement, which merely disposed of the bogey of Article 116 since the two powers mutually renounced claims for war damages, provided for the resumption of normal diplomatic relations and opened the way for an intensification of economic contacts by promising each other most-favoured-nation treatment in such matters. These arrangements in fact mirrored the sort of economic agreements which Berlin had been negotiating with the Baltic countries since the end of 1919 [doc. 6] and it is thus well to point out that the Rapallo agreement is also to be seen in the light of Germany's effort to consolidate its position in eastern Europe. The pact operated on many levels. If a threat to Poland and Franco-Polish efforts could be read into the agreement (72, 78), it acted on the other hand in the long run like a magnet to the smaller eastern European states by providing one of the few constants in a confused period, and suggesting that their own future welfare lay in playing an accommodating role in the development of German-Russian economic contacts rather than becoming too enmeshed in alliances against these two powers.

Opinion of all parties except one in Germany reacted favourably to the implication that the Rapallo agreement was an important step on the way to Germany's recovery, nationalists conveniently overlooking the difference in ideologies between the republic and the first communist state. Such differences of course earned the 'Rapallo policy' the dislike of the SPD, fearing thus an increase in KPD influence as well as not wanting to alienate Allied opinion (59). Yet the events of 1923, when France invaded the Ruhr, simply confirmed what Wirth and all other realists knew, that the useful German-Russian connection could never be an end in itself. During the inflationary and political crisis of 1923 the Russo-German 'alliance' helped to remove the threat of possible simultaneous Polish action in the East to complement the French invasion of the Ruhr (70, 72). It could solve neither the reparations crisis nor the other problems of Versailles as Wirth's double-edged policies had shown. In this sense Stresemann benefited from his predecessors' efforts and it is not surprising that the Ruhr crisis contributed to the process, which we have considered, of 'liberating Stresemann from the views of a narrow, conservative partisan politician' (54).

Stresemann, who became Chancellor for a brief period beginning in August and thereafter dominated German policy as foreign minister until his death in 1929, followed the aims of all previous German officials in seeking to revise the Versailles treaty. Whether one accepts that his policy was a variation on the 'fulfilment' policies of Wirth, in its attention both to East and West (87) [doc. 7], or whether one believes that his emphasis on 'partial revision' was quite novel (5), attention must be given to the vastly changed circumstances in which Stresemann had to operate. Of the greatest importance, the shocking social and economic effects of the Ruhr crisis had prepared the Allies to consider Germany's difficulties more carefully, seen at its most striking in the replacement of the discredited Poincaré by the new French leader, Edouard Herriot who was in principle prepared to co-operate with Germany. Yet the French, with their inferior numbers and potential, still needed security against a future resurgent Germany, particularly since the effects of the Rapallo pact on Poland in 1923 had thrown into grave doubt the usefulness of France's eastern allies. Hence the importance of Stresemann's recognition of the need for conciliatory moves towards France. 'A solution of this (security) question without Germany', he warned, 'would be a solution against Germany' (91).

Economic stability and the solution to Germany's currency problems were an absolutely essential prerequisite to the success of Stresemann's policy (see chapter 5) for these provided the more normal conditions for lengthy diplomatic exchanges. Thus by 1925 Stresemann was at last in a position to reopen an idea that Chancellor Cuno had raised prematurely in 1922, that of a security pact with the Allied powers. Such a pact was achieved with the conclusion of the Locarno treaties in October 1925 and their eventual signature in London on

1 December 1925. These were agreements pivotal to Stresemann's whole policy (77). On the one hand the Locarno settlement provided for an outright acceptance by Germany of her western borders, those with Belgium and France, and mutual guarantees to this effect were to enter into force (as were the other arrangements for the East) when Germany became a member of the League of Nations. This arrangement went far to relieve France of anxiety about her borders with Germany and opened the field for greater co-operation between Germany, France and Britain. There is thus a fairly clear line running from Locarno. In December 1925 the Allies evacuated the first occupation zone on the left bank of the Rhine (chapter 2); in the autumn of 1926 Germany entered the League of Nations, hitherto dominated by France and Britain, which also gave the Republic a greater opportunity to further its policies of support for German minorities abroad; in the summer of 1927 the Allies agreed to reduce their Rhineland occupation forces by 10,000. By 1929 the 'Young Plan' was put into action (chapter 9) and the early evacuation of the Rhineland was on the cards.

If these achievements helped to pull together the moderate parties (chapter 3) the Locarno treaties were bitterly disliked by German nationalists as was any co-operation with the detested League of Nations and thus, ultimately, Stresemann was deprived of complete victory even over his own party (91, 113). This is the more regrettable in that Stresemann also zealously guarded the aim of revising Versailles and this can be seen by looking at the Locarno arrangements for eastern Europe (52, 55, 62). In sharp contrast to his guarantee of Germany's western borders, Stresemann would sign only treaties of arbitration with Czechoslovakia and Poland, thus creating a precedent for the different treatment of the peace settlement in East and West, a more important step in the quest for revisionism than any yet taken. This success would have been inconceivable without the changed European atmosphere after 1923, although it also reflected the aversion of England to extending its commitments to eastern Europe (77) which made matters easier for Stresemann.

It might be asked, if Rapallo had not precluded keeping open options with the West did Locarno mean closing options in the East with Russia? When Germany entered the League might she not have to take up arms against Russia in the event of conflict between that country and another state (Poland for example!) in accordance with the obligations imposed by Article 16 of the League Covenant? Not so. In a note from Great Britain and France to Germany it was agreed at Locarno that a League member could only fulfil its obligations to the League under Article 16 (which provided for sanctions against an aggressor) to the extent 'compatible with its military and geographical situation.' In effect this meant a recognition by the Allied powers of the special relationship which existed between Russia and Germany **(58)**. Thus once the Locarno agreements had been safely negotiated and not a moment before, in spite of Russian pressure **(60)**, Stresemann continued to develop the longstanding contacts with Moscow by signing with Russia the Treaty of Berlin in April 1926. This provided for continuing mutual good relations, clarified Germany's stand vis-à-vis Article 16 and opened the way for further large German credits to Russia.

Locarno and Berlin taken together show not so much a balancing act as the fact that 'East' or 'West' could never individually satisfy Germany's needs after the Versailles Treaty had been signed. In many ways Stresemann simply made more explicit trends in Weimar diplomacy between 1919 and 1923 for the striking feature of that diplomacy at the level of departmental officialdom was its realism. Realism reached, so to speak, a new peak under Stresemann as can be seen by glancing finally at the *cause célèbre* of German nationalists, Poland and its relations with Germany after Locarno. In effect these pacts excluded any effort at a forceful revision of the Polish-German frontiers, a chimera of the nationalists given Germany's military weakness. The Locarno treaties did not of course exclude economic pressure on Poland, as could be seen by the Polish-German trade war after 1925. In this sense the continuing links between Moscow and Berlin remained invaluable **(62, 68, 72)**, although the improving international climate no longer threw Germany and Russia so closely together **(58, 73)**. There is now, however, a great deal of evidence to suggest that, in spite of the inevitable and continuing stress on revisionism against Poland at the level of 'high policy', at the lower level of everyday negotiations, for example over each country's minorities, there was a real effort to find a *modus vivendi* in the changed atmosphere after Locarno **(78)**.

It is impossible to say where these developments would have led, since they depended to a great extent on the ability of foreign ministers to manage the ever present domestic pressures of their nationalists. The force of Stresemann's personality and the weight of his reputation made it possible for Germany to develop a consistent foreign policy between 1923 and 1929 in spite of such pressures [**doc. 7**]. Such was the penalty of Versailles that if it left open room for movement, it remained the easy target for nationalist propaganda and prevented Stresemann from getting full credit for his remarkable policies. Sadly, his death in 1929 coincided with an economic crisis during which the sort of national feelings were aroused that made it even more difficult to achieve a *modus vivendi* at any level.

5 Economics and reparations

If it is impossible to accept that the Weimar Republic's early economic difficulties were caused by the reparations issue, the ill-feeling engendered by this problem produced the sort of uncertainty which was bound to aggravate existing economic difficulties. As a result of an economy isolated by wartime conditions the supply of goods in Germany did not keep pace with the natural increase in paper money, and excess purchasing power, not absorbed by higher taxes, pushed up prices. The abandonment of the gold standard in Germany on 4 August 1914 removed another restriction on the issue of currency and thus inflation was pronounced before the war ended. In 1914 a dollar was worth 4·20 marks, by early 1920, 100 marks. The shock was greater when in 1919 Germany was again exposed to wider economic contacts and the relative scarcity of goods and raw materials resulting from the war effort meant more price increases. The lost resources of the German territories handed over at Versailles included 14·6 per cent of arable land, 74·5 per cent of iron ore, 68·1 per cent of zinc ore, 26 per cent of coal production as well as the potash mines and textiles industries of Alsace. Other losses included merchant ships over 1,600 gross tons, half the merchant ships between 1,000 and 1,600 gross tons, a quarter of the fishing fleet, large quantities of rail locomotives and rolling stock as well as any public property in the ceded territories and colonies, armaments (see chapter 8) and German property in Allied territories **(99)**. The Republic was saddled with a colossal debt incurred from financing the war of some 150 milliard marks, and postwar difficulties in Germany demanded government expenditure on an unprecedented scale. It is in such a context that the reparations problem must be examined.

The Versailles treaty left open the amount to be paid by Germany in reparations to meet the civilian war damages claims of the Allies and the work of determining Germany's total indebtedness was carried out in the Inter-Allied Reparations Commission which began its work on 10 January 1920 and at certain conferences of the Allied leaders.

Meanwhile Germany was to make large deliveries of gold, convertible currency, goods and raw materials. By 27 April 1921, the Commission had set the total of Germany's debt at 132 milliard gold marks and, after the London Ultimatum of 5 May 1921 and in accordance with the concept of 'fulfilment' (chapter 4), Wirth's government made the first large cash payments in August 1921. The rapid inflation which had set in in Germany after the London Ultimatum continued, however, and by the end of 1921 the German government declared itself unable to make the payments due for 15 January and 15 February 1922.

It was already clear to most by this time that reparations were as much a political as an economic issue **(96)**, hence Lloyd George's ambitious plans for a solution in the wider context of a regeneration of the whole European economy and the calling for the World Economic Conference at Genoa. America's insistence on the prompt repayment of its loans to the Allied powers compelled the latter, however, to press Germany harder for reparations **(96)**. The attitude of the French in particular hardened over the reparations issue after the Rapallo 'bombshell'. The Allied case was that it was in Germany's power to effect reforms of the currency and taxation and to stabilise the mark in order to achieve the budgetary surplus for reparations payments. In effect this was to assume that it was deliberate German policy to allow an economic and financial crisis in order to escape unwelcome burdens. Poincaré seized the chance to test his views when he ordered the occupation of the Ruhr in January 1923, after a technical default of German payments in kind, and prepared to force Germany to accept its responsibilities over reparations.

The German view was that reparations had intensified, if not caused, her economic difficulties and some agreement was needed before Germany could stop her spiralling inflation. The Germans had in mind a moratorium on payments and a foreign loan. Two important points arise here. First, whilst the 'non-party' government of Wilhelm Cuno proclaimed Germany's inability to meet reparations charges, they responded to the French occupation of the Ruhr by ordering 'passive resistance', and this cost Germany more than twice the annual charge of reparations which it declared itself unable to make in 1921. Second, the Germans stabilised their currency before a settlement had been agreed over reparations and before getting a foreign loan. After Stresemann's courageous ending of passive resistance on 26 September 1923 a new currency was issued on 15 November 1923, the so-called *Rentenmark*. The crucial question was how far this would command confidence in Germany, since currency needs to be 'covered' and the Reich no longer had sufficient gold reserves or reserves of foreign currency **(99)**. An ingenious answer was the founding of the *Rentenbank* which was endowed with collateral in the form of mortgages of all land used by industry and agriculture. This solution sufficed until the printing of a new Reichsmark at the end of August 1924, and with the circulation of money brought under strict control the German government no longer relied, as it had tended to, on the printing presses of the *Reichsbank.*

These events appeared to substantiate charges of German duplicity and critics rightly pointed out that financial experts like the President of the Reichsbank, Rudolf Haverstein, had made the postwar inflation worse by being too liberal with the issue of credit before the 'collapse' of 1923 **(98)**; rightly, people charged German industrialists and speculators with profiting from inflation, but the failure of the German government to take properly firm action before 1923 can be more reasonably explained by seeing men like Wirth as the victims to some extent of the magnitude and novelty of postwar economic problems. One only has to examine misguided efforts by the German government to carry out tax reforms before 1923, even if there is truth in the charge that they feared alienating the right, to see how inadequately suited were older conceptions to the changed conditions. What use was it, for example, defining taxes 'in terms of nominal money value at a time of progressive currency depreciation' **(99)**? Moreover, the stabilisation of the currency came after Germany had suffered a traumatic crisis [docs. 8, 9] and when the need for unpopular decisions was demonstrably clear, a factor not sufficiently stressed when one remembers that German leaders had to justify policies to parties and pressure groups who treated the Versailles terms as unwarrantable. Finally, it has to be recognised that Germany's internal solution to its inflationary crisis in 1923 was a temporary one and depended on further arrangements at an international level. As much was recognised when in October 1923 the American President, Calvin Coolidge, supported the proposals leading to a new plan for reparations which took its name from the chairman of a committee of experts, Charles Dawes. The Dawes Plan, in force from 1 September 1924, was in itself provisional and sought to lessen the political dangers inherent in the reparations issue by ensuring that Germany's future reparations payments were of a scale which would neither prevent the balancing of the German budget nor lead to inflation. A moderate scale of payments was fixed, rising in five years from £50 million to a standard rate of £125 million, and a loan of 800 million gold marks was raised, mainly in America, to help finance German payments.

It is now well known that the Dawes Plan 'sounded the signal for a period of recovery the scope and intensity of which were unparalleled in recent German history' **(99, 5)**. This appeared to vindicate the defenders of the harsh economic treatment dished out to the Weimar Republic at Versailles, particularly since much German capital was involved in the ensuing economic upsurge **(17)**. It must be remembered, however, that this recovery owed a great deal to the large amount of foreign aid flowing into Germany between 1924 and 1929, attracted by the prospects for investment in a country whose economic development was also carefully watched over by Allied representatives carrying out the Dawes Plan. If cynics pointed out later that between 1924 and 1930 some 25·5 billion marks flowed into Germany in the form of loans and investment whereas Germany paid, ultimately, a total of some 22·9 billion marks in reparations, nationalist opponents of 'fulfilment' warned of the massive and dangerous debts being incurred and bitterly attacked the Allied controls.

Moreover, German governments were hardly able to ensure that the recovery benefited all sections of German society and thus to remove the dangerous political discontent that accompanied economic hardships. It is true that governmental interference in the running of the economy increased during and after the war, as could be seen by the setting up of the Reichsbank for example or the nationalisation of the Reichsbahn (railway) in 1919, but the failure of the revolutionary leaders to exploit their chances after 9 November 1918 put an end to plans for sweeping measures of socialisation. The constitution spoke merely of the permissible step of socialising suitable private industries **(17)**. The idea of 'autonomous authorities' which included representatives of appropriate sectors of society and which were to carry out nationalisation of coal, potash and steel, for example, in fact came to little in view of the vagueness of the constitutional references **(5)**. The factory councils, which according to a law of 4 February 1920 were to play a central part in the running of enterprises of over twenty workers, were disappointing. If they helped in pacifying feelings they were effectively controlled by the unions and thus part of the wider clash of interests between employer and employee. The direction of all economic enterprise remained therefore the 'exclusive right of the entrepreneurs' **(17)**.

Employers were bound to gain some advantage on the whole from the economic expansion after 1924, for by 1929 industrial production had surpassed the prewar level. Of note was the increase in the number of large concerns or 'cartels' of which there were over 2,000 in Germany by 1930, in spite of anti-cartel legislation by the government in November 1923. Yet the shock of 1923 left a lasting horror. If industrialists like Stinnes had been able to profit for a time from the inflation to pay off massive debts in worthless currency, the working masses and salaried employees, functionaries of one sort or another as well as those who had lent money at fixed interest, had all been hit hard. The general effect was to transfer wealth from the thrifty, cautious sections of the lower middle class to the industrialists and financiers **(31)**. Moreover, high unemployment levels in the later 1920s marred the 'prosperous' Germany and could not be wholly compensated for by the general rise in workers' earnings. In any case the latter were affected by rising prices **(95)**.

Nor did the situation in agriculture give cause for satisfaction. German agriculture had of course suffered from the exhausting effort to supply Germany's wartime needs in the face of the Allied blockade, which was reflected in the low crop yields of 1920 and the diminished livestock. The situation of the small farmer was made more intolerable by the absence of the sort of sweeping land reform that was the rule in eastern Europe after 1919. Some 20 per cent of cultivated soil in Germany belonged to 0·7 per cent of proprietors. The *Reichssiedlungs-gesetz* (Reich Settlement Law) of 29 January 1919 foresaw the possibility of expropriating estates over 100 hectares to facilitate settlement but it proved impossible to overcome the resistance of the landlords, and in particular of the powerful Junker aristocracy east of the Elbe, which was represented by the DNVP. Thus between 1919 and 1928, only just over 500,000 hectares were freed by the settlement law benefiting a mere 2·4 per cent of the German farming population **(5)**. The losses of 1923 compelled small farmers to borrow at exorbitant rates thereafter. Moreover, agricultural prices rose more slowly than those for industrial products, of which the farmers were consumers and the profits from the excellent harvests of 1928 and 1929 were offset to some extent by the high world prices. If the Nazis were the hope of the white collar urban workers it is not surprising that rural support was also important to Hitler's movement **(109, 131)**, and in general the economic pressures in Weimar Germany go far towards explaining the difficulties in forming coalitions (see chapter 3) as well as the growing appeal of extremist parties (see chapters 6 and 7).

Few people think rationally about cause and effect in economic crises and what has happened to them must be somebody's fault, invariably the government's. Truly stable societies can weather such storms, but grave difficulties were bound to arise in Weimar Germany when the economic crisis of 1929 interacted with a political and social crisis during which vociferous opponents of democratic government could coin potent slogans and capitalise on the growing resentment against the Republican leaders.

6 Leftist opposition

The continuous pressure from the left and right of the political spectrum made working compromise in government infinitely more difficult to attain since during the Republic the German Communist Party (KPD) and the Nazis (NSDAP) were always in opposition. It was, moreover, a destructive opposition in that both movements were essentially anti-parliamentarian, although both contested elections – the KPD from 1920 onwards, the NSDAP after 1923 – and both movements generated further harmful ill-feelings by being violently opposed to each other [doc. 19]. Since one important element in the ultimate success of the NSDAP was its constant exploitation of the 'communist threat' [doc. 13], the weaknesses of the KPD are of obvious interest to the historian. That the KPD would be anti-Republican is explained by recalling that it sought specifically to rectify the development of the German revolution at the hands of the SPD leaders; that the impetus towards founding the KPD was primarily intellectual, for the voting in the workers' and soldiers' councils had shown the lack of a mass following for communism (see chapter 1), ensured also that the debates about how best to combat the new Republic were vitriolic, and these internal divisions, echoing the longstanding tensions within the German Social Democratic movement as a whole, marked even the founding congress of the party between 28 December 1918 and 1 January 1919.

The new party formed during these days joined the Spartacists to the so-called Left Radicals, who were centred on Bremen and had branches in North Germany, Saxony and the Rhineland and excluded the USPD whose leaders, for all their differences with Ebert and his colleagues [doc. 2], still temporised on the questions concerning Germany's future development (100). This break in itself demonstrated the pressure from the leftists in the KPD with which Rosa Luxemburg had to contend. If she was deeply interested in the example of the Bolshevik seizure of power in Russia, as was evident in the programme she drafted for the KPD early in 1919 (5), her plans for restructuring German society had little room for terror of the Russian type and they

37

postulated a prolonged and necessary period for the education of the German masses. This entailed avoiding precipitate action and contesting elections to the National Assembly in order to reach a wider audience. 'Your activism may seem simple and easier', she warned the delegates who had just founded the KPD, 'but our tactics envision a longer road' **(100, 103)**. Sixty-two delegates against twenty-three voted to boycott the coming elections and subsequently Luxemburg died as a result of the failure to hold in check those members who were still intoxicated with the Russian victories of 1917 and who, in spite of the evidence, felt they could be imitated in Germany.

Looking back it is possible to see 1925 as the turning point in the history of the KPD, when Russia's influence on it became paramount, but between 1919 and that year the party followed its 'zigzag' course **(39)** between those who, like the new leader from 1919–1921, Paul Levi, sought to continue Luxemburg's effort to overcome the KPD's isolation in German politics and to broaden its base, and the 'leftists' who still refused to abandon the 'putschist' tactics that had cost them so dear in 1919. The failure of the KPD to play any significant role in the 'high point of working class solidarity' – the demonstrations that helped to put an end to Kapp's effort in 1920 (see chapter 7) – reinforced Levi's arguments. At least the party contested the elections to the first Reichstag and by April 1920 the ultra leftists had been forced out and had organised themselves into the *Kommunistische Arbeiter Partei Deutschlands* (KAPD) which rapidly thereafter lost political influence **(100)**. Yet it was Russian influence that made the weak and ineffectual KPD into an important force. At the Halle Congress of the USPD in October 1920 the party split on the issue of whether or not to join the Third International or Comintern, the Russian sponsored organisation to keep foreign communist parties in line with Moscow's policy and interests. Under the pressure of Zinoviev, the Russian president of the Comintern, who spoke at Halle, 296 delegates voted to join it against 156 and by December 1920, more than half the USPD members joined the KPD. For the first time it became a mass party with almost 400,000 members, thirty-three daily newspapers and strong positions in the trade unions **(39, 90)**.

Levi's view of the KPD, which entailed preventing it from being dominated by the Comintern, was, however, certain to earn him the animosity of Moscow and thus to strengthen the continuing efforts of the leftist members of the party. The party's central organisation, or *Zentrale,* was situated in Berlin, where the important leftist leaders like Ruth Fischer, Ernst Reuter and Arkadi Maslow wielded most influence. After Paul Levi's resignation from the chairmanship of the

Zentrale in January 1921 along with his supporters, his successor Heinrich Brandler was less able and willing to counter leftist pressures for direct action, which thrived in the jubilant mood created by the realisation that the KPD was a mass party. At the same time the Comintern emissary, the former Hungarian dictator Bela Kun, arrived in Germany to urge direct action by the KPD to alleviate Russia's current difficulties. The Bolsheviks were then in the process of negotiating the Treaty of Riga with the victorious Polish state. The outcome of such pressures was the 'March Action' of 1921 in Central Germany where the communists hoped to exploit the internal crisis occasioned by the Allied occupation of the three Rhine ports (see chapter 5). The result was another fiasco and the rapid suppression by Reichswehr and police of the revolt in Saxony. Quite decisive in the failure of the KPD effort in March was the lack of support forthcoming from the masses **(100,105)**. Public opinion was bitterly hostile and membership of the KPD fell to just over 180,000. Levi's subsequent public disavowal of action by the *Zentrale* action in March led to his expulsion along with other 'rightist' sympathisers from the KPD.

Ironically, putschist policies no longer suited Lenin, who had accepted finally after the Polish-Soviet war that the spread of communist revolution was by no means inevitable in the immediate future, and who, in the interests of attracting foreign aid and consolidating the revolution in Russia, had introduced his New Economic Policy (see chapter 4). Thus the Third Comintern Congress in Moscow in late June–July 1921, provided the occasion to discuss the failure of the March action and to effect a new Comintern line. In accordance with this it was the intention of the new leadership of the *Zentrale* of the KPD under Ernst Meyer to forego direct action and to aim for a united front of German labour, although pressing for drastic measures of socialisation. The new 'rightist' policy was not modified in 1923, underlining again the ineptness of the KPD tactics **(105)**. In the year of the Republic's most severe crisis not much was done by the KPD beyond their participation in the Social Democratic governments in Saxony and Thuringia.

Hasty military preparations were made in October under Comintern pressure but by this time the crisis was nearly under control. The Reichswehr easily deposed the governments of Thuringia and Saxony and the KPD, in the obvious absence again of mass support, could achieve nothing, thus suffering a 'relatively bloodless but ultimately most decisive defeat' **(100)**. Within months Russian control of the KPD was to become even tighter. After Lenin died on 21 January 1924, the triumvirate of Stalin, Kamenev and Zinoviev were struggling to establish their control in Russia against Trotsky and it became more important to secure the unconditional support of non-Russian communist parties. In effect this meant tightening the Bolsheviks' control over the leaders of foreign parties. This led logically to the leadership of the KPD by Ernst Thälmann from 1925, a man who was completely submissive to the Russians and to Stalin.

The KPD ended its *Kampfzeit* (time of struggle) and assumed its definitive form at a time when the Weimar Republic was stabilising itself internally and externally. The KPD's declared policy of 'concentration of forces' **(39)** implied both awaiting a future struggle and yet, whilst proclaiming itself not reconciled to the Republic, continuing to contest elections with some success and playing an opposition role in the Reichstag, as well as working inside the trade unions. Yet this necessary concern with 'practical politics' in a period of relative stability could never gain for the KPD the sort of following that would make revolution a feasible proposition in Germany. The ill-conceived struggle to seize power by force between 1919 and 1923 had merely isolated the KPD from the majority of the working masses, at least those employed, for whom the traditional effort to alleviate conditions by bargaining had infinitely more appeal. Broad sectors of working-class society were in any case alienated by the excessive control exercised by the Comintern over the KPD. Right up to its downfall in 1933 the KPD failed to win over a clear majority of the German industrial workers in spite of rapid gains during the crisis and the trade unions remained 'bulwarks of reformism' **(2, 90)**. The efforts of the KPD widened the gap between itself and the SPD and thus lessened the chances of effective political resistance against the Nazis after 1929 as has so often been pointed out **(2, 29)**. In any case, the 'bolshevisation' of the KPD after 1923 entailed a tightening up of the whole party structure which left no room for the sort of flexible tactics necessary to reunite the working-class movement in Germany and which tolerated only the type of leaders who would submit to the bureaucratisation of the party.

It is thus indisputable that, unable to control the working-class movement in Weimar Germany, the KPD weakened it. The KPD can hardly in itself be blamed for the original defects in the SPD leadership, but its activities further inflamed moderate party, as well as nationalist, opinion against the socialist movement as a whole and thus further reduced the freedom of movement of the SPD, so fateful after 1929. In this sense the KPD's development reflected the obsessively selfish concern of the other Weimar parties with sectional interests. Ironically, when the KPD appeared to be more of a serious threat during its

Kampfzeit, conservative and anti-republican groups in the Reichstag were arguably less inclined to push their opposition to government policies to extremes, whereas such restraint was less apparent after 1923 when the KPD's day to day activities possessed simply a potential nuisance value. Stability and a reduced threat from the KPD thus perhaps weakened the basis of democracy **(109)** (see chapter 3 also), particularly since rightists and National Socialists persisted in identifying the communists as a scapegoat for the pressing problems of the Republic. Either way, for most historians, it appears that the KPD could do no right.

Perhaps it is indeed time, as was pointed out in a recent article **(105),** for the more redeeming features of the KPD to be examined. The passionate devotion to the ideals of the KPD which its supporters brought, penalised as they were by economic hardship and unemployment, helped to offset the bureaucratic rigidity of the party organisation. This membership fluctuated wildly and bore a relationship with the current economic and political development of Germany but one of its strengths, as was pointed out by a German observer in 1932, was precisely its criticism of the German economic and political system **(90).** Preparation for more forceful opposition had not of course ceased after the failures of 1923 and one must note finally the significance of the KPD's paramilitary force, the *Roter Frontkämpferbund,* formed by Thälmann in 1924. Unlike the other similar force formed to fight the opponents of the Republic in 1924 the *Reichsbanner Schwarz-Rot-Gold* **(6),** which rapidly developed into a force of the SPD, the KPD's force was later able to play an important role in the defence of the working classes against the Nazi street gangs and, with its two associated groups, the *Rote Jungfront* and *Rote Marine* had already reached a membership of some 100,000 in 1924 **(5).**

7 Rightist opposition

In turning from 'leftist' opposition, one is immediately struck by the depth, range and variety of rightist opposition to the Weimar Republic as well as by the force of its ideological traditions. At one level was the opposition of the powerful conservative forces of Wilhelmine Germany, which the revolution had failed to break, manifesting itself in the DNVP as will be seen below, in the Reichswehr (chapter 8) and in the authoritarian civil service, bureaucracy and judiciary, not to mention the Church. The anti-Republican sentiments of these authorities could result in a less than impartial repression of communist or left wing activities and a markedly more lenient treatment of the Freikorps leaders or of Hitler in 1923 **(133)**. This was furthermore a bureaucracy, the function of which was all the more important in view of its continuous day-to-day activities during the more turbulent periods of party political struggle. At another level was the opposition of the numerous Freikorps and paramilitary groups which thrived in early postwar Germany, rejecting the return to organised life and unemployment (chapter 8), but which were also called on at key moments to support the Republic. At another level again were the numerous *Völkisch* groups which had their roots in the prewar period and which the National Socialist German Workers' Party (NSDAP) came to dominate **(115, 129)**.

The difficulty of drawing strict lines between the segments of the rightist opposition is indeed shown by referring briefly to the values implicit in the term *völkisch*, the stress on German race and purity, the exaltation of specifically German characteristics and the pronounced antisemitism. They were shared by the rightist opposition, particularly in view of the general radicalisation of right wing thought effected by the bitter experiences of the First World War **(107, 111, 123, 130)**. The existence of a powerful, potentially explosive mixture of discontent, resentment and sheer frustration on the right was indisputable, at its most extreme form demonstrated by the three hundred or so political murders which took place in Germany between 1918 and 1922 **(133)** [doc. 11]. How to use this force for more specific and constructive ends was quite another matter.

The only available political party at first for the nationalists was the DNVP and the strengths and shortcomings of this movement are therefore of obvious interest. The DNVP, founded in November 1918, was the heir not only of the two former conservative parties of Wilhelmine Germany but of the Christian Socialists and of the prewar racist and antisemitic organisations like the Pan German League (117). The largely Protestant dominated party sought specifically to become a mass party, made up as it was from a thorough mixture of social groups, and to achieve 'the organisation of all forces that wished with a holy seriousness for the real reconstruction of our downtrodden fatherland on the basis of traditional values' (113). In effect the DNVP was held together chiefly by its negative attitude towards the Republic and, in accordance with its monarchist outlook, its policy between 1919 and 1924 was one of outright opposition, relying, if anything, on the rather unrealistic hope that it might gain power hand in hand with forceful action by the Reichswehr (117).

By 1923, however, such a negative outlook came to seem pointless in particular to important economic pressure groups associated with the DNVP. Over half the party's Reichstag members belonged to the powerful organisation of landowners, the *Reichslandbund* (29), and these, for example, saw participation in government as a means of fighting for agrarian tariffs; the smaller industrial representation in the DNVP was interested on the other hand in the economic prospects offered by the Dawes Plan (29, 89, 113). These pressures argued in favour of responding to DVP overtures for the DNVP to join the government (see chapter 3). Moreover, the various right-wing efforts to seize power or overturn the government, Kapp in 1920, Hitler in 1923, had been suppressed and the head of the Reichswehr, Seeckt, had not made a decisive move to seize control. The DNVP leadership under Count Kuno Westarp was thus bound to respond to the pressure of many DNVP supporters to take an active part in government and to work from inside to change a state which was abhorrent to them. At the same time, the diehard sectors of the party, whose spokesman rapidly became Alfred Hugenberg, continued to urge all-out opposition.

In 1924 the internally weak state of the party was made plainer when fifty-two of its Reichstag deputies voted for Dawes and forty-eight against. The 'realists' had their way when the DNVP participated in first the Luther then the Marx cabinets, but such promising trends towards the DNVP being assimilated in the party system of the Republic were never allowed to develop in view of the constant resistance from the extreme right wing of the party and its associated extra-parliamentary groups. Their views seemed vindicated by the fact that the mere presence of the DNVP in Weimar governments did not bring about either the desired economic developments (see chapter 3) or a reversal of Stresemann's foreign policy. Thus Westarp's difficulties were acute, whatever his own personal defects in leading the party. After the electoral reverses of 1928 were interpreted by the right of the DNVP as the result of working with the detested middle parties, the way was open for Hugenberg to become First Party Chairman. Unlike Westarp, he had little inclination to do the splits and opted decisively in favour of keeping the support of the more rampant type of national-ists. The man, who brought his money and powerful press to his cause, wrote in 1928: 'I believe in a government by the elect few, not by the elected. . . . I believe in leaders, not in speakers. Words are enemies of action. . . . I believe in government by strong men who have the will power and the strength to carry out national decisions' **(113)**. Hugenberg's version of the *Führerprinzip* which was bound to lose him in time the support of large sections of the DNVP, may be seen as the result of the party's failure to reconcile the pressures from its extreme supporters with the dictates of office, which demanded give and take with the other responsible Weimar parties.

The NSDAP, which had been founded in 1919 and which Hitler rapidly came to dominate, did not of course have this particular prob-lem since it remained in opposition until Hitler came in not just as a member of a coalition, but to play the central role in the government formed in 1933. There are more than enough readily available books on Hitler's rise to make a chronological description of this superfluous in a study which offers merely an analysis of some of the problems of the Weimar Republic. An obvious starting point is to consider the effects of Hitler's abortive 'march on Berlin' in 1923. The fiasco of this year reinforced Hitler's determination that the NSDAP must work to become a truly mass movement and this entailed concentrating on electoral activities and following the 'legal' road to winning a majority of voters. It is useful to stress that for seven years these tactics brought virtually no return in terms of significantly measurable increases in electoral support, the NSDAP gaining a mere 2·6 per cent of the votes cast in the 1928 elections. What is of significance, however, is the way in which all this time Hitler further clarified the priorities of his move-ment and refined and extended the organisational bureaucracy of his party, a process which goes far to explain how he could best profit from the successful electoral breakthrough of the movement when it came in due course. It goes without saying that the very effort to concentrate on electoral campaigns required a streamlining of the party's organisation, but of possibly greater interest is the vital connection between the very nature of the support Hitler sought to attract and the distinctive organisational form of the NSDAP, with its emphasis on the all-seeing, all-powerful Führer **(2, 109)**.

This can best be understood by stressing that the NSDAP was based not only on protest but on resentment. This can be seen from its 'programmatic' utterances, which will be considered below, as well as the character and background of Hitler's chief followers and party officials. Hitler, of course, incorporated in his own person the chief features on which his movement thrived, the frustration, the hate against Jews and Marxists whom he often shrewdly identified with each other, the dislike of parliamentary democracy, dissatisfaction with his position in society **[doc. 13]**. To create a mass movement from such beginnings and to hold it together required unique personal qualities, and it was clear from the very beginning of the NSDAP that it depended above all at first on Hitler's magnetic oratorical ability, as can be seen from the fact that of forty-six NSDAP gatherings between November 1919 and November 1920, Hitler appeared no less than thirty-one times as the chief speaker **(109)**. An interesting circular process soon became apparent. The greater the range and diversity of support for Hitler and the more potent his appeals became for refuting the existing order, the more crucial became his status as the sole leader capable of holding together such diverse elements. In turn the 'dynamism of the movement' and 'its 'fanaticism and rejection of any compromise' justified his growing insistence, particularly after his emergence from prison and the party's refounding early in 1925, on his unconditional authority as the Führer – a 'superhuman force' – at the apex of a strictly hierarchical party structure **(128)**; in turn this gave him the power necessary to adapt his tactics to the exigencies of the moment and thus, like some mathematical progression, to extend still further the appeal of his movement. As early as 1921 he was able to force through within the party his views on the uniqueness of the NSDAP amidst the welter of postwar *völkisch* groups. So much so that the growth of the still small party from 27,000 in 1925 to 108,000 in 1928 resulted chiefly from its absorption of most of Germany's racist and *völkisch* groups, as well as followers from the very young and from such Freikorps units as *Oberland* and *Wiking* **(112)**. Thus by 1929, and given the state of the DNVP, the NSDAP was virtually unrivalled in its hold over the extremist right in Germany.

Hitler, however, needed the sort of organisation that could control more than the extremists on the right and it was therefore of the greatest importance that he should persuade his fellow party leaders to accept his newer, omnipotent image after 1925. Although attempting to become a mass movement, the NSDAP remained essentially anti-parliamentarian and at its inner core a conspiratorial movement **(90)** **[doc. 12]**. Hence the importance of Hitler's choice of fellow conspirators, who would in time be able to manipulate a mass following under his direction. The basis of the movement for Hitler's purposes had to be Bavaria, a base which had already provided him with important contacts with higher officialdom prior to 1925 and where, in the atmosphere engendered by memories of the 'red revolution' of 1919, his appeal was obvious **(28, 29)**.

It was vital that other groups formed outside Bavaria would accept their control by party headquarters in Munich. Yet, given the fact that Hitler was forbidden to speak publicly in most of Germany after 1923, the extension of the NSDAP was greatly dependent on the initiatives of local and regional party and SA leaders. In the conditions of hardship and struggle during the lean years between 1925 and 1930 Hitler needed leaders who had the ability to command local followings and hold their own against rivals. An analysis of the *Gauführer* of the NSDAP shows older men, mostly grown up before 1914, with extensive but generally incomplete educational backgrounds, not from a purely proletarian milieu and with a record of having either fought for a period in postwar Freikorps or border defence units and who had often failed in an effort to return to professional life **(109)**. Clearly, such men as Gregor Strasser, the party's leader in North Germany, or Julius Streicher in Nuremberg who made up the 'old fighters' of the early NSDAP movement were never disposed to accept entirely the increasingly impersonal structure of command which accompanied Hitler's elevation to the level of a mythical figure, way above the party bureaucracy but with the right to interfere anywhere and at any time in the functioning of that machine **(128)**. Hitler's effective control of their criticism, stemming from their acceptance in the last resort of his personal power in the movement as a whole, could never entirely eliminate lingering resentments. This applied even more to the *Sturm Abteiling* (SA) which had been originally founded in August 1921 as the party's paramilitary body to keep order at meetings and make party propaganda and which was reorganised in 1925 and began wearing its brown uniform in the same year. The replacement of its original leader Ernst Röhm by Franz Pfeffer von Salomon in 1926 reflected Hitler's determination to make the SA confine itself to supporting the political organisation and to limit its tendency to behave like other Freikorps units as a revolutionary and often almost autonomous fighting force. Again, Hitler was never entirely successful in suppressing the revolutionary mood in the ranks of the SA **(109, 110, 112)**, which became more troublesome after 1930.

On the whole Hitler's control of his party offered a staggering contrast with that of other party leaders of the Republic, with the notable exception of course of the KPD. The KPD, however, based itself on a class struggle whereas the NSDAP appeared in fact classless. This, paradoxically, derived from the flexibility of movement which Hitler achieved with his iron control of the party machinery. It enabled him to widen continually the scope of his propaganda and appeal and in doing so, incidentally, to disguise the truly revolutionary nature of his movement. The party's original programme was presented early in 1920. Its twenty-five points showed the 'National' side of the movement for all to see in its rejection of the peace treaties, in its call for the union of all Germans in a 'Great Germany', in its racist stress on 'German blood' as the test for membership of the German state and thus its rejection of all Jews. Its 'socialist' side was displayed in its concern for the state with the individual's work and welfare, in its demand for profit-sharing in the 'great industries', in its talk of nationalisation of businesses and its references to land reform in point 17, in the interests of the community as a whole, although such anticapitalist terms were considerably played down later on in the years before the seizure of power. Hitler often, in his early speeches, spoke proudly of his originality in coupling 'National-Socialist' together **(118, 119)** and indeed the programme is symptomatic of the deliberate attempt to exclude no support that might be forthcoming in Germany. In 1926 the Party's programme was declared immutable in order to stifle internal conflicts, which simply deflected energy from the movement towards power, but an earlier and acute contemporary observer of the German scene remarked of the programme: 'In spite of their (the terms) decreed immutability they are neither clear nor binding for purposes of practical policy' **(90)**.

In other words, policy was to be decided in practice by Hitler, and his tactics were always influenced by the desire to command the maximum following. The force of his movement derived after all from its dynamic criticism of the existing order, its negations of the *status quo*; 'It is best to assume these negations as the solitary, definable position. With them the movement became great' **(90)**. Needless to say, the antisemitic basis of Hitler's propaganda remained pronounced, as did the stress on the communist menace; the virulent rejection of party politics and parliamentary democracy **[doc. 13]** continued, as did the violent denunciation of Germany's external enemies. The most striking example of Hitler's ability to reorientate the movement in the interests of its growth is, however, the way in which he switched his main effort from the urban working classes to the rural population between the end of 1927 and early 1928. He had hoped to achieve his mass support from the working classes by drawing an attractive picture of their place in the future *völkisch* state towards which the movement was working **(125)**. 'What we want is not a state of drones but a state which gives to everyone that to which on the basis of his own activity he has a right' **(119)**. Concentration on winning over the urban masses could also be reconciled with the Nazi denunciations of democracy, since presumably massive Nazi support in the towns could in theory have produced the sort of revolutionary movement whose sheer weight, as was the case in November 1918, would have crushed the existing order leaving the way free for the mass party to rule **(2)**. The fact remained, however, that the NSDAP signally failed to win over to any extent the working-class supporters of the SPD and the KPD in spite of renewed efforts after 1930. Thus Hitler instituted his 'rural-nationalist' plan, seeking to exploit the growing discontent among the small farmers of the countryside (chapter 5). His control of the party was demonstrated beyond all dispute, for this change of emphasis meant 'nothing less than an organisational revolution' **(128)** for the movement, the redrawing of the different *Gaus* in which party structure existed to coincide roughly with the boundaries of Reichstag electoral districts. To establish the fact that Hitler was both leader and 'programmer' of the movement, the change of tactics brought a further 'clarification' of point 17 of the party programme of 1920. It was explained that 'expropriation of land for communal purposes without compensation' did not mean that the NSDAP was against private property but that the clause referred merely to property illegally acquired or not used in accordance with community interests, i.e. by 'mainly Jewish speculators' **(125, 128)**.

It was only with the dramatic breakthrough in 1930 that the dividends of Hitler's refusal to commit himself irrevocably to a programme drawn up in any detail were seen to be an advantage. Then it was possible to see that the sudden and massive increase in numbers was indeed, in economic terms, rooted in the 'panic' of the German middle classes **(2)**, whom the Republican parties had so disappointingly failed to convince that they would effectively guard their interests **[doc. 19]**. If there were longstanding 'traits' of German historical and intellectual developments which predisposed certain sectors of German society towards Hitler's movement, this brief analysis of some of its general features simply confirms how important it is also to give full weight to the general crisis in Germany after 1929, for only then did Hitler's gamble pay off; and it was a gamble, not only because the world economic crisis could hardly have been predicted but because there was also a danger that, in generating a movement which concentrated primarily on acquiring power, it would be progressively more difficult to control unless it achieved power. It should be added, however, that Hitler's tactical skill in widening the appeal of his movement must not be allowed to obscure the remarkable consistency of his own viewpoint *(Weltanschauung)* and long-term aims. The implications of this, unfortunately, were rather more clear after 1933 than before.

8 Reichswehr and politics

Ebert's failure to exploit his power properly had led him to rely on the old German army to keep order and the officers of that army saved their own skins, strengthening their foothold in the new Republic by helping Ebert to crush his political enemies on the extreme left [doc. 14a]. That this process was not easy to reverse was confirmed by the law of March 1919 on the provisional Reichswehr (as the new German army was called). Although this specifically referred to the army being formed on a 'democratic basis', it was difficult to see how this could be achieved since the law also in effect recognised the *status quo* by permitting the recently formed Freikorps to form the basis of the Reichswehr, under the control of the old officers (138). Essentially anti-Republican forces thus formed the core of the new army. Its structure was further determined by the military provisions of the Treaty of Versailles, which eventually became law in Germany once the treaty was accepted. According to the treaty the army was to be composed of seven infantry and three cavalry divisions under no more than two army corps headquarters. The army was to be made up of no more than 100,000 men, serving for twelve years except for up to 4,000 officers who were to serve for twenty-five years. No more than 5 per cent of the effective forces were to be replaced each year. The army was to possess no offensive weapons, no aeroplanes, no tanks, and other weapons permitted to Germany were listed in detail. The celebrated Great General Staff was to be abolished, as were the military academies and cadet schools. All measures of mobilisation or preparation for mobilisation were forbidden as was the manufacture or import of poison gas and other war materials. Any weapons surplus to those permitted by the Allies had to be handed over in due course. Similar detailed provisions were made for the German navy including the express forbidding of submarine manufacture (5, 138).

These measures clearly revealed the Allied distrust of the German 'militarism' and of the powerful traditions of the old German officer corps. The German army, the first unified army in Germany's history, since the once separate contingents and military authorities of the separate states no longer existed under the new constitution, was thus clearly to be restricted to a virtual 'police' force, enough to keep internal order but not to wage another war. Not the least important implication of the Versailles military terms, however, was that they made it even more unlikely that the Reichswehr would undergo future 'democratic' reforms. The emphasis on a small professional army, a reflection of the Allied fears about the former mass levies of prewar Germany, attracted the rightist Freikorps mentality rather than the republican moderates, for want of a better term; the fact that Germany was to be allowed only a small army seemed to argue leaving it in the hands of those who knew best how to make the most of it, the officers of prewar Germany.

Uneasy relationships between the Reichswehr and the Republic were almost certain since the world of the officer corps had been that of personal allegiance to the Kaiser and a highly privileged position in German society **(138, 139, 140)**. The Republic was hardly 'doomed at birth' **(146)** because of its reliance on the officer corps, since much depended on personalities and on future developments. Early conflicts however, gave an idea of the problems involved. There were few officers, though they existed, who were ready to share the readiness of Walther Reinhardt, the first Chief of the Army Command, to co-operate closely with the Republic. With such a man, Gustav Noske, the Minister of Defence, might have had some hope of integrating the Reichswehr into the Republic, but in 1919 Reinhardt became increasingly isolated not only from his fellow officers **(138)** but from the Freikorps leaders, who continued to nurse the hope of direct action against the Republic. The resentment of the Freikorps formations **(112, 135, 138)**, many of whom faced unemployment in view of the reductions in the armed forces demanded by Versailles, led to the so-called Kapp Putsch in 1920.

After the refusal of the commander of the Reichswehr district which included Berlin, General von Lüttwitz, to disband the radical Erhardt brigade, this particular Freikorps formation marched into Berlin on the night of 12–13 March. The cabinet was forced to leave the city and a 'government' under Lüttwitz and Wolfgang Kapp, a former Prussian civil servant, was set up. In point of fact, Kapp was in time isolated not only by a universally hostile public opinion and by the general strike called against him, but by the response of the key Reichswehr leaders. Reinhardt was virtually alone in wanting the Reichswehr to put down the rebels, but while the attitude of the other officers towards Kapp was ambiguous to say the least **(138)**, and certainly not positively in favour of the Republic, in the last resort they put the unity of the army above Kapp, whose action threatened to split it beyond repair. Deprived of effective support, Kapp eventually fled the country and Bauer's government came back to Berlin.

The Putsch showed the futility of frontal attacks on the Republic but Noske's efforts to integrate the Reichswehr into the Republic were discredited, and the gap between SPD and army leaders widened. How imprisoned the SPD leaders were in their conceptual framework was shown, however, by the fact that, far from exploiting the divisions in the Reichswehr, they followed with devastating logic the consequences of their original reliance on the old army leaders and replaced Reinhardt – 'the one General who was prepared to defend the Republic by force of arms' (138) – by a man whom they believed would have the confidence of the officers and men, General Hans von Seeckt, a man whose activity as Chief of the Army Command between 1920 and 1926 gave the Reichswehr its definitive structure. In 1919 Seeckt had been head of the so-called *Truppenamt*, which in effect exercised the functions of the now forbidden General Staff. Like Reinhardt, Seeckt accepted the need for co-operation between Reichswehr and Republic but had no time for integration. Put another way, the Reichswehr would tolerate the Republic for the time being in its own interests. Reichswehr and government were, so to speak, coalition partners, both sharing a concern for stable political developments since civil war threatened the unity of the state and that of the army. As Seeckt had in effect urged in response to suggestions to put down Kapp, 'Reichswehr does not fire on Reichswehr'. Such internal conflicts had to be avoided at all costs in the interest of concentrating all energies on the long-term objectives of restoring Germany's greatness and fighting the war of liberation against the Versailles powers. It followed for Seeckt that the spirit of discipline, unity and obedience of the old German army could best be fostered in the Reichswehr by building a 'Chinese wall' around it to protect it as far as possible from outside influences (138, 142). It followed too, that only the supreme leaders of the Reichswehr could concern themselves with politics. This was the real meaning of the 'non-political' Reichswehr and it demanded, in a time of excessive interest in politics, that the mass of the Reichswehr be politically neutral and simply obedient [doc. 14b]. The mark that Seeckt's work left on the Reichswehr will be understood by looking at its structure of command and its composition, as well as by examining its attitude to important political events.

A prerequisite for Seeckt's policies was to secure for the Chief of the Army Command the necessary power since neither the Versailles Peace, nor the German constitution nor the law on the army (*Wehrgesetz*) of 23 March 1921 provided for the sort of supreme military leader that Seeckt wanted. The key lay with the Minister of Defence who was permitted to exercise the supreme command over the Reich's military forces by the Reich President, in whom the command was vested. The fact was that Seeckt's personal ascendancy over the Defence Minister who succeeded Noske, the Democrat Otto Gessler, produced a reversal of the roles originally allotted to the Chief of Army Command and Defence Minister. In practice Seeckt took all important military and political decisions in the Ministry of Defence and thus, although not himself answerable to the Reichstag, gained access to cabinet meetings and to the President, whilst Gessler was more or less reduced to covering up for the Reichswehr in the Reichstag and in public as the 'responsible' minister. It is true that after Seeckt's resignation Gessler tried to redress the balance by taking advantage of the lesser personality of Seeckt's successor, General Heye, but then had to reckon with the growing importance of his own nominee in the new Wehrmacht department, Kurt von Schleicher, who had already gained his experience under Seeckt. Groener's arrival at the Defence Ministry in 1928 naturally reduced the importance of Heye, but Groener relied heavily on Schleicher who, from 1929 the head of the new *Ministeramt* in the Defence Ministry, exercised the political powers which only Seeckt had been able to combine with military powers. The latter were wielded by Heye's successor in 1930, General Kurt Freiherr von Hammerstein-Equord, a man who had 'close personal links with Groener and Schleicher going back over many years'. Thus the influence Seeckt had secured for the military in his own person remained in the trinity of Schleicher, Groener and Hammerstein. The close links persisted between the top Reichswehr leaders and the President [doc. 16] and minimised, as Seeckt had desired, the area of contact between Reichswehr and Republican institutions (138).

The alienation between Reichswehr and Republic can of course also be seen by examining the composition of the army which is in turn connected with the Freikorps formations of postwar Germany. The political outlook of these was rightist, composed as they were of professional officers and NCOs of the Imperial army, and their resentment against the Republic made them thoroughly disruptive factors in postwar Germany. The sympathies of the Reichswehr leaders also lay with the right in German politics, but the success of Seeckt's policies depended on avoiding a repetition of the Kapp Putsch, which might provoke premature action and a split in the Reichswehr. Nor did the emphasis of the Officer Corps on discipline and tradition have room for the extremism of the Freikorps formations and of the group loyalty of these to their own leaders [doc. 11]. Yet the Reichswehr had been based on the Freikorps formations and it was precisely from such circles that the Reichswehr could find most of its recruits, given the refusal of the officers to select men from the left. Thus, although the Freikorps were dissolved after the Kapp Putsch, they continued to exist in underground or terrorist groups such as *Organization Escherich (Orgesch)* or *Organization Consul* and were partially reconstituted in 1923 (112, 133). Indeed they formed an essential pool of reserves in times of crisis since they also possessed extensive arms and equipment. An illegal 'Black Reichswehr' was a useful way of avoiding some of the limitations of Versailles and, although at the end of 1923 Seeckt again sought to draw a clear line between the Freikorps formations and the regular troops, the love-hate relationship persisted and particularly close co-operation eventually developed between the Reichswehr and the largest and most important group, the *Stahlhelm*. This contrasted markedly with the gap between Reichswehr and the Reichsbanner, which had been set up in 1924 by the SPD deputy in the Prussian parliament, Otto Hörsing, specifically to rally Republican forces against such groups as the Stahlhelm (6). Such a state of affairs could be expected given the extraordinarily conservative nature of the officer corps which still relied on the traditional recruiting grounds of the old Prussian force, the sons of former officers and of the professions and which had on average 21 per cent of its officers from the nobility, although these formed a mere 0·14 per cent of the German population (138, 139). Given their choice, recruits would continue to come from paramilitary circles, even if such contacts led them into conflict with civilian, and particularly Prussian, authorities. Even after the resignation of Seeckt, when slightly better relations existed between government and Reichswehr, the former not the latter went more than half way to legalise an illegal procedure by closer financial control of the 'black' funds, which totalled 3,380,000 marks in 1928–29 and which came increasingly from public money, rather than from the private contributions of agriculture and industry on which Seeckt had relied (5).

Such dubious relationships were but the reflection of Seeckt's self-imposed task of watchdog over 'German' interests and of his constant activity in high politics, all of which made it difficult to work towards a more soundly based relationship between Reichswehr and state. His political ambitions were manifested from the very moment the Republic came into being and for some time ran parallel with those of the DNVP (chapter 7). In 1923 he perpetually harassed and eventually secured the resignation of Gustav Stresemann, the leader of the government of the day trying to deal with the grave crisis facing Germany. His action against leftist risings in 1923 contrasted with his delay in suppressing the Bavarian separatists in that year because this would have meant Reichswehr. firing on Reichswehr. Only Hitler's unsuccessful move, crushed by the police, saved Seeckt from the need to act, and it remains a depressing fact that his possible move against the constitution was thwarted when Ebert shrewdly placed the responsibility for defending the Republic squarely on Seeckt's shoulders by giving him emergency powers on the night of 8–9 November. 'The fiction', a German historian neatly commented, 'that the Reichswehr was the trustee of the state thus became a legal reality' **(140).** If Seeckt's prompt relinquishment of his emergency powers on 1 March 1924 – to the chagrin of the DNVP – did add to the Reichswehr's standing in official circles, it is probable that Seeckt acted so to leave himself free to offer himself for the President's position once Ebert's term of office ended **(138).** These were all extraordinary steps to take for the leader of a state's army, as was Seeckt's determined insistence on the primacy of German-Russian relations **[doc. 15]** in the face of Stresemann's wider political strategy (chapter 4).

Seeckt's views on the political role of the army survived his own resignation in 1926 after the uproar over the participation of the eldest son of the Crown Prince, William, in the exercises of Infantry Regiment Nine. Admittedly the possibility of the army playing a more constructive role in the Republic seemed less remote in the relatively stable period after Hindenburg became President in 1925, giving the Reichswehr a focal point in the Republic. Heye and Schleicher desired a degree of rapprochement between Reichswehr and Republic which was a considerable advance on Seeckt's *attentism* but their view of the nature of the army remained essentially the same. Rapprochement still did not mean integration. If greater public attention was focused on the doings of the Reichswehr, the SPD continued to pay the penalty of its earlier errors, and its attacks on the Reichswehr remained isolated incidents rather than the expression of any concerted effort to force the army towards more constructive reforms **(2).**

It had of course been clear earlier that peaceful coexistence between Reichswehr and Republic was not enough to weather any serious crisis with safety and 1923 had proved that when the interests of political and military leaders seemed opposed there was a danger of direct action by the Reichswehr against the state. The danger was more acute when the Reichswehr leaders faced internal pressures to take action, as Seeckt had found, again, in 1923. That this could even happen testified to the difficulty which Seeckt had of keeping politics out of the

Reichswehr ranks. Given the social composition of the Reichswehr, as well as its pattern of recruitment, it was bound to be more difficult to resist the attraction of the NSDAP as it pushed forwards to the centre of the political arena, and Groener and Schleicher faced the dilemma of Seeckt in an acute form after 1928. In the words of the Social Democrat Julius Leber in 1931:

> I fear the Reichswehr has been built upon a colossal mistake of von Seeckt's. He believed that discipline was enough, and obedience to the commander's will was a sufficient guarantee of the proper functioning of the Army. But no unit in these times will place itself unreservedly in the hands of its commander. The links between the soldiers and the public are too intimate for that and far too closely concerned with social and political trends of every sort **(140)**.

Thus, in spite of army rules to the contrary, national socialism penetrated the ranks of the army through the younger ranks and officers and there found fertile ground to exploit in the growing discontent with an 'a-political' Reichswehr. Such pressures towards 'action' could not be ignored indefinitely by the army leaders as the crisis was soon to show.

One might finally ask what sort of fighting force had been built up as a result of the policy of the Reichswehr leaders, since the desire to prepare for a future war of liberation had been a major justification of their actions after 1918. Clearly, the refinement of the structure of authority in the Ministry of Defence after 1920, the contacts with Russia developed after 1921, and consolidated after the Rapallo treaty, and the persistent links between Reichswehr and the paramilitary forces on the right meant that, in the face of Allied efforts at inspection and control, the core of a more powerful army existed than was necessary to fulfil the policing functions which it had been assigned by the Versailles terms. Through the innocuous sounding *Truppenamt* in the Ministry of Defence were exercised the functions of the illegal Great General Staff and the future army leaders of Nazi Germany gained their experience. Technical developments were made possible through the Russian connections, of special importance being the German flying base operating in Lipetsk after 1924, where fighter pilots were trained and where valuable testing and technical innovation took place. A tank school was opened at Kama by 1929. More systematic cooperation and training links were eventually established between the Reichswehr and some of the paramilitary groups, in particular with the Stahlhelm, whose flying groups were used in 1932 to 'launch a *Wehrflug-*

organisation which combined all the trained flying personnel outside the army'. The power of expansion of the Reichswehr as far as manpower went was thus considerable. What was still needed was equipment. By early 1931, for example, there were still only six medium and four light tanks, although plans had been drawn up for their increase. Great advances had of course been made with the air force and at the end of 1930 the decision was taken to create a secret force of aeroplanes in direct violation of Versailles. The gap still remained between plans and achievement. In 1931 there were still only 29 reconnaissance planes, 15 fighter planes and 26 night bombers, but the number of pilots trained at Lipetsk alone in 1933 was 120, and this gives an inkling of potential developments **(138).**

PART THREE

Conclusion

9 The crisis and Hitler

Implicit in this study has been the assumption that no single problem 'caused' the downfall of the Weimar Republic, but that the interaction of these problems, many of which pre-dated the Republic, progressively weakened the new German state **(9)**, and that, for specific reasons which will be examined in this conclusion, the process reached its climax in the crisis of 1929–33. From this viewpoint the novelty of these years is in part a question of degree. The gravity of the political crisis could already be gauged by the difficulties of Herman Müller, the Social Democrat who was Chancellor between June 1928 and March 1930, in forming a cabinet which would command sufficient support in the Reichstag, notwithstanding the superficially favourable election results of May 1928. Thus Müller's 'Great Coalition' emerged from the device of a 'cabinet of personalities' who could hope to use any influence they had with their respective parliamentary delegations in order to get together a majority to support the government on at least vital issues but could not bind those delegations to the government in any formal way [**doc. 17**]. Perhaps this state of affairs followed on logically enough from what was said earlier about party politics but the class conflict which the 1918 revolution had failed to solve and which underlay coalition difficulties was now aggravated by a mounting financial and economic crisis.

The force of this statement can be seen by examining briefly the internal state of those parties represented in the 'Great Coalition', the SPD, the Democrats, the DVP and the Centre and BVP. Of the Democrats, loyal supporters of the Republic, it is enough to remind ourselves of their remorseless decline which the May elections confirmed. The Catholic camp lost votes too at these elections but from Müller's viewpoint the ominous sign was the replacement of Marx, who resigned the leadership of the Centre, by Monsignor Ludwig Kaas in December 1928. His victory at the expense of the rival candidates Joseph Joos and Adam Stegerwald, who were both close to the Catholic labour movement, confirmed the swing to the right that was remarked earlier.

Undoubtedly, however, the most striking illustration of the proposition that parties reflected the unresolved class conflict was the confrontation between the DVP and the SPD **(19)**. It was obvious that by 1929 only Stresemann's personality was holding the DVP from sliding finally to the right, whereas Müller's own position was made difficult not only by the growing pressures from the Reichstag faction of the SPD but from the trade unions and from the leftist opposition groups within the party. These grew more troublesome after 1925 and captured some 35 per cent of the votes on the debate about coalition parties and armaments at the Magdeburg Party Congress of 1929 **(19)**. The polarisation of political principles was accentuated not so much yet by any threat from the extreme left or right (which was not acute even when Müller fell) as by its very existence during the economic crisis. In 1928, true to its subservience to Russia, the KPD changed its tactics to complement Stalin's own internal struggle and broke off what collaboration had existed with the SPD, branding the latter as 'Social Fascists', thus both confusing political issues and increasing Müller's problems **(2, 39, 105)**. On the right Hugenberg exploited his position as leader of the DNVP to organise the 'National Opposition' against the recent Young Plan after setting up in July a committee representing his own party, the Stahlhelm, the Pan German League and the NSDAP.

This radicalisation of politics, in part pre-dating the economic crisis, significantly circumscribed Müller's actions by making more difficult working compromise between factions; which in turn made it more difficult to tackle the crisis quickly; which in turn completed the vicious circle by intensifying interparty disputes on how best to solve economic problems [doc. 18]. As we saw, economic difficulties were never entirely overcome in the 'prosperous' period. Germany's failure to develop an active trade balance, the decline in tax revenues and the increased expenditure on unemployment insurance through the Reich Institute for Unemployment Insurance which had been set up in 1927, all combined to produce and keep budget deficits **(12, 17, 99)**. The Young Plan, which was put into its final form at the Hague Conference in August 1929 did indeed free Germany from the irksome restrictions of the Dawes Plan and paved the way for the final, if posthumous, act of Stresemann's diplomacy in the evacuation of the Rhineland in 1930. Yet it was certain to affect the financial crisis. The plan contained a fifty-nine-year schedule of reparations payments averaging 2·05 billion and permitting possible deferment of two-thirds of the annuities though under stringent conditions. The fact that all German funds were in future to come from the general budget clearly indicated the expectation that Germany would continue to prosper. Once, however, the celebrated Wall Street Crash of 1929 opened the way for the flight of capital from Germany and Europe, the reparations payments created intolerable strains on the already creaking Reich finances, not least because they appeared to render more difficult the devaluation of the German currency as a possible solution to the economic and financial crisis **(19, 28)**.

In itself this fact made more potent the appeal of the virulent nationalist mood, whipped up by the extreme right both against the Young Plan and against cooperation in general with the Allied Powers. If Brüning faced the brunt of this pressure when he became Chancellor a fortnight after the formal acceptance of the Young Plan by the Reichstag on 12 March 1930, Müller's difficulties pointed the way. The more open conflict of class interests (already 2·5 million were unemployed in the winter of 1928–29 and over 3 million the following winter) entailed the frightened clinging to principles and the consequent refusal to assess properly the increased damage being done to parliamentary institutions, as constant bargaining and negotiations accompanied each successive effort to find an agreed legislative basis from which to tackle the economic crisis. Thus the failure of first Hilferding, the SPD Minister of Finance, and subsequently Moldenhauer, of the DVP, to frame acceptable proposals. Moldenhauer's suggestions early in 1930 might have temporarily solved the problem by including, among other provisions, the raising of the contributions for unemployment insurance from 3½ to 4 per cent, but it was precisely over this issue that the DVP and SPD refused to budge from their respective class interests, the former insisting on rigid economies in this field, the latter, notwithstanding Müller's efforts, protecting themselves against what was felt to be an attack on the very principle of social legislation **(19)**. Thus Müller admitted defeat once it was clear that Hindenburg would not back his government with emergency powers. With the return of the SPD to opposition went the last chance to form a government with a parliamentary majority.

Heinrich Brüning, still only forty-six, a former frontline officer in the First World War, who had risen rapidly in politics to become leader of the Reichstag faction of the Centre Party in 1928, took up the Chancellorship during a period in Germany of profound public disillusionment with the democratic system, and he headed a minority government containing representatives of the parties of the Great Coalition except for the SPD. Ever since his actions have been the subject of heated debate. Much of the argument has turned on Brüning's dissolution of the Reichstag in July 1930 after his government's programme for tackling the economic and financial crisis was repudiated by 256 to 193 votes. By this act he opened the way for the staggering NSDAP electoral successes in the September elections. Those who have criticised this step and his subsequent reliance on the dreaded Article 48 to govern by emergency decrees have regretted that he threw away other chances to secure a working majority **(2)**, in particular that of accepting the eventual overtures of the SPD to compromise over details in the programme. One may ask, however, for how long would such a compromise have been effective. Brüning was, at the very least, limited by the fact that Hindenburg was only willing in the last resort to support a rightist government with emergency powers **[doc. 16]**. This could hardly be concealed by terms like 'presidential cabinet' or 'cabinet above the parties', and Brüning's protectionist policy towards agriculture, effected with the aid of the DNVP Minister for Agriculture Dr Schiele, which kept the price of bread and cereals abnormally high during a period of ruthless economies, reflected the bias of the new government.

In any event the class conflict continued to haunt Brüning as it had Müller. Moldenhauer, Brüning's first Minister of Finance, was compelled to resign in the face of the refusal of his own party (DVP) to accept his proposals of June 1930 for taxation increases. In fact one of the fundamentals of a relatively stable parliamentary system in the Republic, namely a degree of willingness to compromise between the bourgeois parties and the Social Democrats, had apparently ceased to exist when Brüning took office. Moreover, a rapid solution was essential **(40, 41)** since the budget deficit went from 400 million marks in April to 1·1 billion at the end of May. Thus the dissolution of the Reichstag may well have been the undesirable but probable outcome of Brüning accepting in the first instance the unenviable task of heading a 'presidential government'.

These difficulties remain even if it is accepted that Brüning was predisposed towards an authoritarian approach to Germany's problems through a government basing itself on the more moderate rightist forces in Germany. Such an approach, which had room for an eventual restoration of the monarchy, sought to capitalise on the members of the DNVP who had been driven to leave the party in the face of Hugenberg's extremism and who had formed themselves into the Conservative People's Union under Gottfried Treviranus. It was hoped by Groener and Schleicher as well as by Hindenburg that this party would grow into the 'big nationalist, though co-operative party that was their dream' **(17)**. Casting his net towards the more moderate right, and this again entailed keeping the support of the DVP, also made Brüning reluctant to increase his authority by merging the federal with the Prussian government, which was still based on the 'Weimar Coalition'. Perhaps Brüning's scepticism about the possibilities of formulating any constructive policies with the SPD was justified in view of the continuing criticism of that party by recent historians (29, 39).

Be that as it may, the election results of 14 September 1930 changed the situation drastically. Brüning's hope of extending his parliamentary base towards the right was smashed by the fact that the Conservative People's Union returned only four members, by the continued refusal of Hugenberg to co-operate although his party lost thirty-two seats and of course by the massive increase of the NSDAP to 107 seats in the Reichstag. The panic flight to political extremes in reaction to the continuing crisis was confirmed by the gains of the KPD as well as by the losses of the DVP and Democrats, a point which will be further clarified shortly, as will the failure of the government to attract the support of the new voters when the crisis is examined from Hitler's viewpoint. Brüning was therefore racing against time and mounting pressure from the extreme right. His prime aim, however, was not to crush the NSDAP by a frontal assault, which Schleicher would not have permitted (138), nor to involve them in government, but to carry out his plans for financial and constitutional reform and his foreign policy and, by restoring order and sanity, to undermine the appeal of the extremists. He was at first secure in the support of the President and Reichswehr, and in the Reichstag the SPD's panic at the National Socialist gains led them to adopt the policy of 'toleration' towards Brüning. Whilst absolving the SPD leaders from any blame attached to the harsh policies put forward by Brüning, their toleration ensured that the Reichstag ratified the decrees which Brüning passed with greater frequency.

Brüning's remedy for tackling the crisis rested on a rigid economic orthodoxy and was certain to be harsh. It sought to offset the effects of falling tax receipts and to cut expenditure, as well as finding additional sources of revenue. This led to the addition of some ten new taxes and the drastic reduction of the salaries and pensions of government employees in three stages by the end of December 1931. Price cuts of 10 per cent were made. There was further curtailment of the expenditure on social insurance benefits and a pegging down of wage levels to those of 1927. The attempts to balance the budget had the effect of cutting down production to 60 per cent of what it had been in 1928 and in itself this helps to explain the catastrophic figures for unemployment which reached five million early in 1931. The 'one-sided policy of deflation' (39) was at least in part due to the

65

restrictions of the Young Plan against devaluing German currency, and this in turn helps to explain the insoluble link between Brüning's external and internal policies.

If the end of his deflationary policy was to demonstrate Germany's incapacity to pay reparations and by ridding the Republic of such obligations to make palatable the severe domestic measures **(40)**, this aim was made doubly necessary by the inflaming of nationalist sentiments by the 'National Opposition'. Brüning was, however, ultimately dependent in this respect on the goodwill of the Allied Powers, and this was made questionable precisely by his demonstrative efforts to appeal to the rising tide of German nationalism. It was indeed Utopian to expect to satisfy the National Opposition by concessions to militant revisionism **(29, 55)** since for them the continuing attack on Versailles was but part of the attack on the government, but Brüning himself hardly created this dilemma. Hence his espousal of the abortive Austro-German customs union, the forbidden Anschluss in poor disguise, and his effort to achieve equality for German armaments. Not until the last moment, however, was Brüning let off the hook over reparations by the Hoover moratorium of 20 June 1931, on intergovernmental debts, and this only after the alarming rise in the flight of capital from Germany. Some 3·5–4 billion of gold and foreign currency left the country between September 1930 and July 1931 **(17, 93)**. Only after Brüning's fall were reparations effectively ended following the Lausanne Conference in July 1932, and only in December of that year was Germany's right to equality of armaments at last recognised.

Brüning's tragedy was that, however near to success he was on his terms, his policies helped to maintain the conditions in which extremist opposition flourished and this in turn alienated Hindenburg, the Reichswehr leaders and the other powerful forces of German conservatism. The significance of this remark can be appreciated by examining these years from the viewpoint of Adolf Hitler and his movement.

More than any other party the NSDAP depended on the crisis for its successful growth. The official statistics for membership of 1935 show an increase from 129,000 in 1930 to 849,000 by the end of January 1933 **(109)**, while during the crisis years the National Socialists recruited a private army for the SA which reached nearly 300,000 men **(112)**. As to the election results themselves, these clearly revealed the rapid growth in the appeal of the NSDAP for a wide variety of groups defecting from the older parties, as well as for the large number of young new voters who voted for the first time in 1930. While the Catholic vote showed its characteristic resistance to the charms of the

Hitler movement and the SPD lost relatively little support, defections from the nationalist camp, the DVP and the smaller parties representing interest groups all showed the 'panic of the middle-classes' **(2, 22)**, so often remarked on in general studies of Nazism and since confirmed by specialised regional analyses **(106, 125)**. Sociological studies of party membership after 1930 confirm the pattern emerging prior to this. No less than 43 per cent of new members entering the party between 1930 and 1933 were aged between eighteen and thirty and 27 per cent between thirty and forty years old **(109)**. Quite undeniable is the preponderance of the *petit-bourgeois* social groups. White-collar workers, artisans, merchants, shopkeepers, civil servants and so forth were twice as strongly represented in the NSDAP than in proportion to their position in society as a whole, whereas manual workers were markedly under-represented **(112, 131)**. Of those almost 270,000 workers who did join the party before 1933, 120,000 to 150,000 of them were unemployed **(109)**. In the universities too, the National Socialists made great gains **(33, 112)**.

The party derived in particular enormous benefit from their continued effort to win over the rural population in view of the mounting effects of the crisis on agriculture. In general the countryside fell more easily to the Hitler movement than the larger industrial areas and towns, for on the land even the isolated bankrupt had frightening implications for the smaller communities. The success of the NSDAP was striking in Schleswig-Holstein, for example, where between 1928 and 1930 the traditional defender of agrarian interests, the DNVP, fell back from 23 per cent to 6 per cent, while the National Socialists increased their share of the vote from 4 per cent to 27 per cent **(109)**. Such figures help to substantiate the assertion that above all 'it was the victims of the crisis not only the unemployed but the disinherited in general who flocked to the party' **(112)**. At the same time, the movement began to attract the attention of the great landowners for whom Hitler now had a different face and for whom the NSDAP was the lesser evil as it became clearer that its original programme for land reform would not be implemented. Under the influence of Hitler's skilful words the great Agrarian League (*Landbund*) proclaimed its intention in January 1931 of henceforth co-operating with the National Socialists **(112)**.

If the attitude of the industrialists towards Hitler and his movement was initially more reserved, notwithstanding Hitler's efforts to win their support, for example through his celebrated speech to the *Reichsverband der Deutschen Industrie* (National Federation of German Industry) in January 1932, and notwithstanding the support of individual influential industrialists like Schacht and Fritz Thyssen, these were increasingly disturbed by first Brüning's and then Schleicher's policies and this tended to work to Hitler's advantage.

The conflicting interests of these varied social groups were hardly to be reconciled after 1933, let alone before, and thus the movement's failure to clarify its multipurpose programme was confirmed in one sense as a positive advantage. To vote for Hitler was for many, if not most, above all a rejection of the existing system, and an expression of belief that during a worsening crisis Hitler's movement offered the only real hope for the sort of change which specific social groups could fondly hope would be in their interest rather than in those of rival groups. Hence the need for Hitler to focus attention more than ever on the task of becoming the head of government. This was in itself an admission also of the difficulty of controlling the internal tensions of the movement as it became a mass phenomenon. In Hitler's election speeches and in the party's main paper the *Völkischer Beobachter* the earlier propaganda themes of antisemitism and racism were played down **(137)**. They gave way to a 'massive defamation' of the government, a concerted attack on the bankrupt parliamentary system and emphasised the national humiliation of the German state, promising revision and expansion in foreign affairs, as well as pressing the fanatical anticommunist themes, which appealed to so many of the German bourgeoisie and higher social groups **(108, 109)**.

Hitler's rôle as the all-powerful Führer did indeed reach its climax with the massive popular votes devoted to him from 1930 onwards but, as his efforts to woo the agrarian and industrial establishment indicated, there was a potential danger of his 'legal' tactics being undermined by the continuing revolutionary mood running through important sectors of his movement, which were inflamed precisely by its dramatic growth. The danger was highlighted for Hitler in his continuing difficulties with the SA, over 60 per cent of whose members were permanently unemployed and whose bloody street battles with the communists graphically reflected their desire for revolutionary frontal attacks on the Republic. In the late summer of 1930 Hitler was compelled, after an SA rebellion in Berlin, to assume himself the position of highest SA leader and subsequently to reappoint Röhm as Chief of Staff of the SA. The loyal SS under Heinrich Himmler became a separate force and helped to keep order among the SA, but this hardly solved the problem, and the longer the crisis lasted the more difficult it was for Hitler to restrain the activists **(110, 112)**.

How important this was becomes clear by emphasising that, as in the early years of the movement in Bavaria, the NSDAP was not in a position to accomplish a revolutionary seizure of power based exclusively on National Socialist forces and at no time was the movement's share of the vote enough to bring it an absolute majority. This helps to explain the importance to Hitler of effectively disguising the revolutionary purpose of his movement in the later years of the Republic in the way mentioned above. It explains too the importance to Hitler of his alliance with the DNVP in the 'National Opposition', first against the Young Plan and soon, after further meetings between Hitler and Hugenberg in the summer of 1931, against the Weimar system as a whole. This working alliance with the conservative forces in the National Opposition, formalised so to speak in the Harzburg Front after the meeting of October 1931 between the various rightist and paramilitary forces, brought the National Socialists money, the respectability they had certainly not had before and vastly increased opportunities to penetrate the establishment. Yet despite this support, although the NSDAP broke into governments of the Lands before 1933 (Thuringia in January 1930, Braunschweig in late 1930 and Anhalt, Oldenburg, Mecklenburg in 1932) **(109)**, Prussia held out as the bastion of democracy under its Weimar coalition until after Brüning's fall. Even after the Land elections of April 1932 in most of the states had deprived the remaining moderate governments of their majorities, the 'National Opposition' gained a majority only in a few small states **(5, 17)**. Nor could the working partnership between the Centre and SPD in the Reichstag be sprung open between 1930 and 1932 and the hardening mood in the SPD masses was reflected in the preparations of the Reichsbanner from September 1930 to organise a more efficient fighting force. By the end of 1931 the 'Iron Front' had been set up by the SPD, the free trade unions and the workers' sport organisations to oppose the Harzburg Front **(39)**. Yet the protection or at least the tolerance of the influential conservative forces, so vital to Hitler's success, could fortunately for his movement have a more direct influence on events through the exclusive ring of intimates surrounding the ageing and senile President Hindenburg.

This becomes more than obvious by stressing that for Hitler the protestation of 'legality' was specifically directed, as the crisis developed, at securing for himself the powers which Brüning had virtually institutionalised; that he, Hitler, should head a government appointed by the President and be entrusted with extraordinary powers under Article 48. For Brüning, perhaps, there was the justification that he was using emergency powers to preserve the 'state of law', since democracy had clearly failed, whereas Hitler would have no such scruples. The fact remains that between 1930 and 1932 the Reichstag passed twenty-nine relatively minor bills, as opposed to 109 emergency decrees that were ratified by the President. Such an extensive use of these powers and one, which by even depriving the Reichstag of the supervisory role to which it was entitled under the same Article 48 by the threat and act of dissolution in the event of parliamentary disapproval, made habitual a state of affairs that had been originally envisaged as temporary (2, 29). This both accustomed the public at large to think in authoritarian terms of a solution to Germany's problems and helped to effect the transfer of real power to the state bureaucracy, lacking in sympathy as ever for the parliamentary tradition.

Of more direct importance was the increase in the influence of that other anti-Republican force, the Reichswehr. Schleicher's part in getting Brüning appointed underlined this influence [doc. 16], as did the fact that in spite of Brüning's financial restrictions the Reichswehr budget did not suffer. Needless to say, the Reichswehr leaders viewed the crisis from the point of view of what arrangement best suited the interests and future of the army. At first the army leaders were distrustful of the NSDAP and feared its hold over the younger army officers in particular (138). Such a hold was clear enough at the trial in 1930 of the three young national socialist army officers for treason, because of their assertions that part of the army would not oppose the NSDAP. Yet Hitler's profession when he spoke at the trial of these officers, of following the legal road, played its part in changing army attitudes, as did the early contacts between Schleicher and Röhm in the spring of 1931 and later exchanges between Schleicher and Hitler prior to Brüning's fall (112). There remained too the opportunity to use the SA to supplement the forces of the Reichswehr in the event both of a feared, if improbable, attempt by Poland on the German borders and in the event of Germany being allowed greater freedom to rearm. By January 1932 Groener had lifted the existing ban on taking NSDAP members into the Reichswehr.

Such moves reflected the growing acceptance by the Reichswehr leaders of the need to involve the NSDAP ultimately in government and thus to bring to an end emergency rule by extending support on the right. To them this seemed the obvious way in view of mounting evidence of Hitler's appeal to Germans, which was dramatically confirmed in the elections which took place in March 1932 to determine whether or not Hindenburg should have another term of office. In the first vote in March, Hitler's rival candidacy for Reich President brought him some 30 per cent of the votes polled, and Hindenburg just failed to get an absolute majority. Though Hindenburg's position was secured in the second ballot in early April, the old President had become even more susceptible to intrigues against Brüning. His support of Brüning's government with its intensely unpopular policies had brought him the bitterness of attacks and vilification from the rightist forces who had formerly supported him. Thus he was more ready to accept Schleicher's view that Brüning, with his policy of relying on the toleration of the SPD, stood in the way of a government which would include the NSDAP (41). Schleicher also parted ways with Groener whose ban on the SA of 13 April 1932, in response to demands from Prussia and other states and in the interests of keeping order, threatened to destroy another bridge to the Hitler movement. By the end of May, Schleicher's key importance had been confirmed by the forced resignation of both Brüning and Groener.

Whilst there may still be arguments about the significance of Brüning's appointment for the fate of the Republic, most have agreed that his fall removed the last restraints on the Hitler movement in the sense that his successors were preoccupied to a greater or lesser degree with bringing Hitler more on to the centre of the stage rather than countering his appeal. The moment seemed auspicious enough for Schleicher's plan for a rightist government. Brüning's successor and Schleicher's candidate, Franz von Papen, headed a cabinet whose reactionary composition gained it the title of the 'Cabinet of Barons' and in which Schleicher was at the Ministry of Defence. Shortly afterwards a step was at last taken to remove the potential threat of Prussia. With the Reichstag already dissolved on 4 June 1932 in preparation for new elections and with the repeal on the ban of the SA and SS, the murderous street fights and disorder occasioned largely by the NSDAP and KPD activities were used as the pretext to suppress the Prussian government by military action on 20 July 1932. How far the SPD had been progressively weakened by its political tactics and outlook was shown by its failure to accept the use of force to resist, of decisive importance in a year when politics and elections were fought largely on the streets. The election results of 31 July, 1932 brought staggering successes again to Hitler with his party gaining over 13½ million votes and 230 Reichstag seats. If the Centre and SPD remained firm in the face of both NDSAP and KPD gains, the bourgeois parties were virtually wiped out [doc. 19].

It was precisely at this stage that Hitler's gambler's instinct was put to its severest test. The logic of his movement demanded as ever that he control any government of which he was a part. This was not what either Schleicher or von Papen had in mind and so Hitler remained for the moment outside. Hindenburg, who had allowed Hitler to speak to him on 13 August 1932, was quite against allowing him to head a cabinet with presidential powers and the President was incensed by Hitler's failure to support von Papen's government **(41)**. In fact it was von Papen's lack of popularity, since he had no chance of controlling the Reichstag in the face of the KPD and NSDAP opposition tactics on the floor, that worked in Hitler's favour. This was not by any means immediately apparent, for once von Papen was compelled to dissolve the Reichstag disturbing incidents took place in Berlin before voters went to the polls. A strike of Berlin transport workers against the government was supported with violence by the KPD, but was also joined by the NSDAP to underline its own opposition to the forces of reaction, a clear enough sign of the pressure building up in the Hitler movement. As a recent historian of fascism aptly pointed out, however, Germans had 'voted for Hitler to protect them from Bolshevism, not to bring it closer' **(112)**. The November election results did show the beginning of a swing away from the NSDAP, and bourgeois fears were perhaps reflected in the slight recovery of the DNVP and DVP. Whilst the KPD increased its votes, the sudden check to the hitherto continuous growth of the National Socialists and the signs that the economic crisis had passed the worst stages, combined to produce acute depression amongst the top NSDAP leaders who were also aware of their pressing financial difficulties.

In spite of these setbacks the NSDAP was still the largest party and to govern without the National Socialists was impossible. Hindenburg's resistance to allowing Hitler to head a cabinet still stood and the alternative seemed to be, as Hitler still refused to compromise, von Papen's idea of dissolving the Reichstag yet again and suppressing not only the KPD and NSDAP but other political organisations as a prelude to sweeping constitutional reforms. In point of fact this was no alternative, given Schleicher's fear that the army would be crucified in any such venture. Thus Schleicher broke yet another government by convincing Hindenburg of this fact and, if reluctantly quite logically, himself became Chancellor on 2 December 1932. Schleicher could only be successful, however, where von Papen had not been by winning over at least a percentage of the NSDAP. His total failure to achieve this by exploiting the rivalry between Hitler and Gregor Strasser put Schleicher back to square one. Yet not quite. Schleicher's broader attempt to appease other sectors of German society included placatory moves towards the trade unions by considering employment programmes and repealing von Papen's anti-labour legislation. This further strength-ened the tendency of leading industrialists and agrarian leaders to look more favourably on Hitler and this was made evident by the financial contributions to the NSDAP which were made by German industry, after Hitler's meeting with the still resentful von Papen at the house of the banker von Schroeder on 4 January 1933.

This 'suicidal' readiness of the powerful conservative establishment to hand over key powers to the revolutionary movement led by Hitler **(38, 116, 121)**, was one of the most essential preconditions of his access to supreme power but it is not really surprising that it should have manifested itself most decisively at the very moment the National Socialists were showing signs of decline. Precisely such signs reinforced the naive belief that, if harnessed to a coalition with other nationalist forces, the NSDAP could be effectively controlled in the interests of social classes whose very survival after the revolution of November 1918 was increasingly seen to be incompatible with the existence of a Republic. In short, that the Hitler movement offered the hope of sweeping changes and the eclipse of bolshevism, while permitting the German bourgeoisie at the same time to 'rest assured that order and property would be preserved' **(124)**, a sort of painless revolution of the right.

Who was to prevent this? Hardly the weakened and demoralised forces of the German working classes, nor the army once that Schleicher had been replaced by leaders more ready to accept Hitler's views **(109)**. When von Papen had begun to use the weapons of intrigue against the man who had developed them, Schleicher, it was possible to remove the last remaining obstacle to Hitler's entry into the government, namely Hindenburg's resistance. The President, who was very much in favour of von Papen in any event, was more readily influenced by the accession of his own son Oscar to the von Papen camp and grasped at the apparent chance of creating at last a government which would not be isolated from large sectors of German society. Hitler became Chancellor on 30 January 1933, in harness with Hugenberg's nationalists, flanked by von Papen as Vice-Chancellor and apparently comfortably shackled. To subscribe to this astonishing illusion was to forget what Hitler had been saying for years, to forget the weakened and divided state of the Reichstag parties, which now had to contend with Hitler's deliberate plans to consolidate his personal position, to forget or willingly to ignore the intrinsic possibilities in exploiting Article 48 now that Hitler was at the very centre of government and to forget that much of the German nation was already sickened by the tortuous development of German democracy. How much this cumulative process owed to the decades before the Republic was even founded can only have been hinted at in this short study, but it is still essential to give weight, not only to the nature of German problems between 1918 and 1929, but to the quite specific series of events between 1929 and 1933 in order to counter the assumption that somehow Hitler was 'inevitable'. As a recent historian put it: 'The disintegration of the Weimar Republic and the rise of Nazism were two distinct if obviously overlapping historical processes. By 1932, the collapse of Weimar had become inevitable; Hitler's triumph had not' **(38)**.

PART FOUR

Documents

USPD view of political structure

When the Republic was declared the SPD leaders invited the USPD to join an all-socialist government. The reply, printed here, clearly reveals the effort of Haase and his colleagues in the USPD to ensure that genuine changes would take place in the economic, political and social structure of Germany (see p. 4).

To your communication of 9 November 1918 we reply as follows: The USPD is prepared, in order to strengthen the revolutionary socialist gains, to enter the cabinet under the following conditions: The cabinet may only be composed of Social Democrats, who stand together equally empowered as Peoples' Commissars.

This limitation does not apply to the experts; they are merely technical assistants of the executive cabinet. Each of them will have alongside him two members of the Social Democratic parties, one from each party. There will be no condition for delay attached to the entry of the USPD in the cabinet (to which each party sends three members).

Political power lies in the hands of the Workers' and Soldiers' councils, which are to be called together in a plenary Congress from the whole Reich as soon as possible.

The question of the Constituent Assembly will only become actual after the conditions created by the revolution are consolidated and should thus be reserved for later discussions.

In the event of these conditions being accepted, which are dictated from the desire for a united advance of the proletariat, we have delegated to the cabinet our members Haase, Dittmann and Barth.

(Signed HAASE)

From *'Vorwärts'*, 11 November 1918, cited in G. A. Ritter and S. Miller, eds., *Die deutsche Revolution 1918–1919,* Frankfurt am Main, Fischer Bücherei, 1968, p. 83.

USPD demands for action

By the time this programme was prepared the Spartacist 'rising' had been crushed, the elections to the National Assembly had been held and there was no chance of any government implementing the terms proposed in the following extract. Yet it serves as a reminder of the sort of society that might have been created by the revolution (see p. 6).

The immediate demands of the USPD are:

1. Inclusion of the Councils system in the constitutions. Decisive participation of the Councils in legislation, state and municipal government and in industry.

2. Complete dissolution of the old army. Immediate dissolution of the mercenary army made up of volunteer corps (Freikorps). Disarming of the bourgeoisie. The setting up of a people's army from the ranks of the class conscious working sector. Self government for the people's army and election of officers by the ranks. The lifting of military jurisdiction.

3. The nationalisation of capitalist undertakings is to begin at once. It is to be executed immediately in the sphere of mining, and of energy production (coal, water-power, electricity), of concentrated iron and steel production as well as of other highly developed industries and of banking and insurance. Landed property and great forests are to be transferred to the community at once. Society has the task of bringing the whole economy to its highest degree of efficiency by making available all technical and economic aids as well as promoting co-operative organizations. In the towns all private property is to pass to the municipality and sufficient dwellings are to be made available by the municipality on its own account.

4. Election of authorities and judges by the people. Immediate setting up of a Supreme Court of Judicature which is to bring to account those responsible for the world war and the prevention of a more timely peace.

5. Any growth of wealth achieved during the war is to be removed by taxation. A portion of all larger fortunes is to be given to the state. In addition public expenditure is to be covered by a sliding scale of income, wealth and inheritance taxes . . . .

6. Extension of social welfare. Protection for mother and child. War widows, orphans and wounded are to be assured a trouble free existence. Homeless are to be given the use of the spare rooms of owners. Fundamental reorganisation of public health system.

7. Separation of state and church and of church and school. Public, standardised schools with secular character, to be developed according to socialist educational principles. The right of every child to an education corresponding to his ability and availability of the means necessary for this end . . .

Extract from the revolutionary programme of the Independent German Social Democratic Party (USPD), 6 March 1919, in J. Hohlfeld, ed., *Dokumente der deutschen Politik und Geschichte vom 1848 bis zur Gegenwart.* Berlin, Dokumentation-Verlag, Herbert Wendler, 1951– vol. 3, pp. 24–5.

document 3

A liberal view

When the revolution broke out and the socialists assumed power, the other political parties of the Wilhelmine Empire remained, somewhat stunned, in the background. As it became clearer that the SPD leaders would restore the conditions necessary to hold elections to a National Assembly, the non-socialist parties began to reorganise or to reconstitute themselves to fight those elections. The following extract, written by the editor of the Berliner Tageblatt, *Theodor Wolff, gives some insight into how liberal circles viewed events late in 1918 (see p. 19).*

In the afternoon six gentlemen called at my home; three of them I knew and three I had not before met. They were lawyers, industrialists, a professor, and a university lecturer. They wanted me to take the lead in founding a great Democratic middle class party, and expressed the opinion that on account of my attitude during the war I was in the best position to do this. I had no desire to enter into the question whether they were justified in their confidence in me, but already yesterday and today I had been considering the same plan, and since the deputation consisted of people of distinction, and indecision would have been the worst of all things at the moment, I consented. The middle class is frightened and at its wits' end, not knowing what to do or where to turn; most of them are fluttering like birds who have fallen out of the nest and do not know where to go. They must be found another nest, and those who are simply asking all the time 'What is to happen now?' must be given the courage that comes to them only with being in a numerous company and having something to lean on. For a new free state it is possible so far to count on the Social Democracy and the Centre, and that is numerically a great deal, but not enough. The Social Democracy and Catholicism are incontestably two forces of immense importance, and at present the two of the greatest importance. They not only have great hosts at their back but are now the only compact and well knit bodies in the country. But Germany is Germany and anybody with his eyes open and able to look ahead cannot accept these two strong pillars as enough in the long run to give the needed support to a republic — for the Republic has become the only possible thing. Whether it will have a long life in any case is impossible to say as yet, but if at birth it has only a Social Democratic and a Catholic godfather it will be burdened from the outset with a mass of discontent and hostility, and it will be discredited for almost all who might be won over to it from other camps. Thus it is necessary now to organise those strata of the non-Catholic middle-class who are at all inclined towards democratic ideas, in view of the elections to a National Assembly which it must be hoped will take place — even if it has to be admitted that not everything is good metal that is thus welded together. Naturally large numbers of people will cling to this life-line only in order to escape from the mortal danger that seems to threaten them.

Theodor Wolff, *Through Two Decades*, Heinemann, 1936, pp. 138–9.

Weimar election results

	19 Jan 1919	6 June 1920	4 May 1924	7 Dec 1924	20 May 1928	14 Sep 1930	31 July 1932	6 Nov 1932
Totals on register (in mills)	36·8	35·9	38·4	39·0	41·2	43·0	44·2	44·4
Percentage of voters	82·7	79·1	77·4	78·8	75·6	82·0	84·0	80·6
NSDAP								
Seats	–	–	32	14	12	107	*230*	196
Per cent	–	–	6·6	3·0	2·6	18·3	*37·4*	33·1
DNVP								
Seats	44	71	95	*103*	73	41	37	52
Per cent	10·3	15·1	19·5	*20·5*	14·2	7·0	5·9	8·8
DVP								
Seats	19	*65*	45	51	45	30	7	11
Per cent	4·4	*14·0*	9·2	10·1	8·7	4·5	1·2	1·9
Centre & BVP								
Seats	91	85	81	88	78	87	*98*	90
Per cent	*19·7*	17·9	15·6	17·3	15·1	14·8	15·9	15·0
DDP								
Seats	*75*	39	28	32	25	20	4	2
Per cent	*18·6*	8·3	5·7	6·3	3·8	3·6	1·0	1·0
SPD								
Seats	*165*	102	100	131	153	143	133	121
Per cent	*37·9*	21·6	20·5	26·0	29·8	24·5	21·6	20·4
USPD								
Seats	22	*84*						
Per cent	7·8	*17·9*	0·8					
KPD								
Seats	–	4	62	45	54	77	89	*100*
Per cent	–	2·1	12·6	9·0	10·6	14·3	14·6	*16·9*
Number of deputies in the Reichstag	421	459	472	493	491	577	608	584
Votes cast in millions	30·4	28·2	29·3	30·3	30·8	35·0	36·9	35·5

The figures given for the NSDAP in 1924 are those of the racialists.
Source: G. Castellan (5), p. 117.

German discussion of peace terms

After the elections to the National Assembly, a coalition was formed from the SPD, the Democrats and the Centre Party. The new government, headed by the Social Democrat Chancellor, Philipp Scheidemann, had to deal with many complex and urgent problems. This extract is from one of the cabinet meetings which considered the coming terms of peace. The contrast between this reasoned discussion of tactics and the public utterances of the government is marked (see p. 11).

COUNT RANTZAU: Let me make a few preliminary remarks. Our enemies will submit the completed draft (of the peace treaty) with the words 'Take it or leave it'. The draft will diverge widely from Wilson's programme. There are three possibilities: to turn it down; to make a counter proposal; or to examine the draft in detail and make individual counter proposals. The latter is the right approach. Negotiators must be instructed in such a way that they can offer counter proposals. Wilson's programme leaves untouched the question of freedom of the seas as well as the Schleswig question and that of a German-Austrian union. I have divided the material into ten points for the time being: territorial questions; protection of minorities; reparations questions; trade policies; financial questions; general legal questions; German colonies; disarmament; League of Nations; war guilt.

Reparations questions: Rantzau gives further information

ERZBERGER: We must base our arguments on the note of 5 November 1918. After the formal exchange of notes, according to international law, a treaty was concluded. Belgium will have to be completely rebuilt. This does not hold for Northern France. . . . The principle for the method of payment must be: small quotas extending over a long period of time. . . . There is the possibility that in the long run changes will be made, anyhow. Payment must be in kind, not in money.
DAVID: I agree that we should rest our case on the note of 5 November, but the enemies will have a different interpretation. The note says: 'German attack', not 'German attacks', which means that Germany waged an aggressive war and must make good total damage.

DR BELL: We must take a stand on the guilt question. One might explain that the march through Belgium was motivated by erroneous assumptions. (1) This was an emergency, in which ordinary rules did not apply, and (2) Belgium had a secret agreement with the Entente. We have since realised our mistake. We are, therefore, responsible for repayment of damages.

NOSKE: I still think that in extreme emergencies one fends for oneself as best one can. I cannot even recognise German guilt in Belgium. Nor in U-boat warfare, either – it was a counter measure to starvation blockade. I agree that payments should be spread over a long period.

COUNT RANTZAU: We can justify submarine warfare by the hunger blockade. Other guilt questions will be taken up under point 10.

COUNT BERNSTORFF: The enemies . . . will say: 'Besides Wilson's points it must be taken into account that Germany must be punished.' We can reply: '. . . You only wished to fight to abolish autocracy and militarism and that has been eliminated.' But we won't get anywhere and the big guilt question will still be raised.

GOTHEIN: England and America show understanding for our inability to bear great burdens.

GIESBERTS: We cannot scrape up four billions a year. The standard of living of the German workers and the social welfare measures must be safeguarded. This we must emphasise as a precondition, with reference to the internal political struggle (Bolshevism, etc.).

LANDSBERG: . . . The question of guilt and reparations cannot be separated. The march into Belgium resulted from an emergency, but was not self-defence. Emergency conditions do not relieve us from the responsibility for damages, so we should consent to making restitution. The payments should be small.

EBERT: What is the extreme limit of our capacity for reparations payments?

RANTZAU: Does this imply an authorisation to break off negotiations if demands endanger our very existence?

ERZBERGER: Let us maintain, according to the Note of November 5, that reparations be limited to damage in occupied areas. No other demands should be recognized . . .

COUNT RANTZAU: I agree. The Reich reparation commission

has estimated that on that basis we would have to pay 20 to 25 billions. This takes into account deliveries since armistice and perhaps colonies given up. This sum is within reason. Payments should be in kind.

SCHIFFER: The principal consideration is what we can pay. Granting that domestic obligations and obligations towards neutrals must be met, hardly any resources are left for payment. . . .

BELL: Our negotiators must be clear as to what is the limit of our capacities. . . .

COUNT BERNSTORFF: From the legal point of view, we should stick to our interpretation, but we won't be able to put it across, since the English would then not be entitled to reparations, which they keep mentioning in every political statement. . . .

EBERT: There is agreement that the note of November 5 in its most favourable interpretation should serve as our starting point.

Extracts from the meeting of the Reich Ministry of 21 March 1919, from Burdick and Lutz **(44)**, pp. 268–73.

document 6

Relations with Russia

According to the Treaty of Versailles, Germany was compelled to recognize in advance future, as yet unspecified, Allied arrangements for Russia, yet the following document indicates the possibility of Germany exploiting the vagueness of some of the Versailles clauses. The memorandum was composed during the course of the Soviet-Polish war, towards which Germany's official policy was one of neutrality, a policy which in effect benefited Russia rather than the Poles (see p. 14).

Germany is so far limited in the independence of its Eastern policy by the Treaty of Versailles that it must recognize in advance the settlement of Eastern questions intended by the Entente. So far, in theory, it can conclude with Russia, as with Latvia, only a 'provisional' agreement; also it cannot undertake any alteration of the terms of the Treaty of Versailles, in agreement with Russia, which (country) in this respect is quite unhindered. . . . It is up to Russia to make any

provisional treaty which is concluded durable, by allowing . . .
the Entente no decisions which oppose the agreement concluded or to be concluded with Germany, which the growing
position of power of Russia *vis-à-vis* the Entente makes
possible. For this reason the priority of the German-Russian
negotiations is of significance and suspicions which could
arise against these (negotiations) beginning in view of German
neutrality must be rejected. Economic negotiations are not a
breach of neutrality.

*Auswärtiges Amt Files, Akten betreffend Verhandlungen mit Sowjet
Russland (Graf Mirbach, Ostschutz) Politik 2 Russland, Bd 1*, London,
Foreign Office Microfilm, K281/K095960—K095962.

Memorandum of the Russian Section of the German Foreign Office
dated 13 August 1920.

document 7

Chancellor Marx on foreign policy

*When Marx formed his fourth cabinet early in January 1927, he brought
in the Nationalists on the condition that they accept Stresemann's
continuation in office as Foreign Minister. This hardly led the DNVP
to abandon its hostility towards Versailles or towards the principle of
co-operating with the Allied powers, but it enabled Marx to offer the
following announcement to the Reichstag (see p. 23).*

In no other sphere is the continuity of governmental aims to
a greater degree the prerequisite of fruitful work than in the
sphere of foreign policy. This continuity is the basis of international confidence. Germany would immeasurably increase
the difficulties of its position if the organic development of
its policy towards the other countries were damaged by
changes in internal politics. So it is self-evident that the
government will further develop the existing foreign policy
in the sense of mutual understanding. This line is clearly and
unequivocally identifiable from the decisions taken with the
consent of the constitutional authorities in recent years. The
foreign policy which the Reich government has pursued
unceasingly and unflinchingly since the end of the war and
which ultimately led to the London Dawes Agreement, to the
treaties of Locarno and to entry into the League of Nations,
is characterised by a rejection of the notion of revenge. Its

purpose is rather the achievement of a mutual understanding. Whatever may have been the standpoint of individual parties in the past, for the future the only appropriate development can be that indicated, on the foundations thus achieved. . . .

Extract from the government declaration of Chancellor Marx before the Reichstag on 2 February 1927. J. Hohlfeld, ed., *Dokumente der deutschen Politik und Geschichte vom 1848 bis zur Gegenwart,* Berlin, Dokumentation-Verlag, Dr Herbert Wendler, 1951, vol. III, p. 171.

document 8

Domestic impact of inflation

When the French occupied the Ruhr in January 1923 to force Germany to meet her reparations payments, the ensuing economic and monetary crisis produced shocking and lasting effects on large sectors of German society, as the following two documents 8 and 9 demonstrate (see p. 36).

May I give you some recollections of my own situation at that time? As soon as I received my salary I rushed out to buy the daily necessities. My daily salary, as editor of the periodical *Soziale Praxis,* was just enough to buy one loaf of bread and a small piece of cheese or some oatmeal. On one occasion I had to refuse to give a lecture at a Berlin city college because I could not be assured that my fee would cover the subway fare to the classroom, and it was too far to walk. On another occasion, a private lesson I gave to the wife of a farmer was paid somewhat better — by one loaf of bread for the hour.

An acquaintance of mine, a clergyman, came to Berlin from a suburb with his monthly salary to buy a pair of shoes for his baby; he could buy only a cup of coffee. The Zeiss works in Jena, a nonprofit enterprise, calculated the gold mark equivalent of its average wage paid during a week in November 1923 and found weekly earnings to be worth four gold marks, less than a sixth of prewar levels.

Personal memoir of Dr Frieda Wunderlich, cited in Bry **(95)**, p. 55.

Health and the cost of living

In the session of the Prussian legislature for January 23, the Prussian Minister of Welfare, drawing upon the report submitted for Prussia, has already given us a picture of the most grievous want and deep misery in matters of health in that state.

Unfortunately, this picture of accelerating and shocking decline in health conditions applies to the whole Reich. In the rural areas where many self-sufficient farmers are able to feed themselves and the difficulties resulting from a great density of population do not exist, conditions seem to be better. But in the towns and in the districts with an industrial mass population, there has been a decided deterioration. Especially hard-hit are the middle class, those living on small annuities, the widows and the pensioners, who with their modest incomes can no longer afford the most basic necessities at present day prices. It is going just as badly for those who cannot yet earn. I mention students only as an example. The expense of even the most essential foodstuffs – I need only indicate fats, meat and bread – and the want of coal, linen, clothing and soap, prevent any improvement in living conditions. The height to which prices have climbed may be shown by the fact that as of February 15, wholesale prices have risen on the average to 5967 times the peacetime level, those of foodstuffs to 4902 times, and those for industrial products to 7958 times. Meat consumption has fallen from 52 kilograms per person in 1912 to 26 kilograms per person in 1922. In the occupied zone, moreover, this small amount has presumably to be shared with many foreign mouths as well. For many people, meat has become altogether a rarity. A million and a half German families are inadequately provided with fuel. Thousands upon thousands of people spend their lives jammed together in the most primitive dwellings and must wait for years before they can be assigned quarters which satisfy even the most elementary hygienic requirements. . . .

It is understandable that under such unhygienic circumstances, health levels are deteriorating ever more seriously. While the figures for the Reich as a whole are not yet available, we do have a preliminary mortality rate for towns with

100,000 or more inhabitants. After having fallen in 1920—21, it has climbed again for the year 1921—22, rising from 12·6 to 13·4 per thousand inhabitants. In 1922, those familiar diseases appeared again in increasing numbers which attack a people when it is suffering from insufficient nutrition, when it also can no longer obtain the other necessities of life. Thus edema is reappearing, the so-called war dropsy, which is a consequence of a bad and overly watery diet. There are increases in stomach disorders and food poisoning, which are the result of eating spoiled foods. There are complaints of the appearance of scurvy, which is a consequence of an unbalanced and improper diet. From various parts of the Reich, reports are coming in about an increase in suicides. . . . More and more often one finds 'old age' and 'weakness' listed in the official records on the causes of death; these are equivalent to death through hunger. Just recently the painful news appeared in the daily press that a well-known German scholar, Professor Hayn of Dresden, has died of hunger.

Extract from a speech by Franz Bumm, President of the Reich Department of Health, before the Reichstag on 20 February 1923, in Ringer, ed., **(98)**, pp. 112—13.

document 10

False legends

An eminent German historian recalls his own experience of the early Weimar Republic and gives some idea of how pervasive were the rightist legends of early postwar Germany (see p. 42).

I myself am, perhaps, not the worst witness in this matter since I grew up in the midst of this atmosphere. In our high school in Stuttgart, as, indeed, in most of the secondary schools in Germany after 1918, a noticeable rightist trend prevailed, which most of the teachers followed, at least those who spoke to us about politics. We believed that it was the stab in the back alone that had prevented a German victory; we had one Pan-German history teacher who defended this worst form of the legend. We were convinced that one could be patriotic only on the rightist side. We repeated the stupid jokes, which were then circulating among the middle class, about President Ebert and his wife, and which were supposed to prove their unworthiness. In fact, the Eberts succeeded, with quiet dignity, in regaining a sympathy for Germany under the most trying conditions – in a world in which public opinion was dominated by Germany's wartime enemies. About this, however, we heard nothing, and we read nothing about it in our rightist middle class press. We did not know what the actual situation of the war had been in 1918; we were taught to hate the French and the British and to despise the Americans. We were pressed into a form that had become empty. We did not see that the socialist workers had also sacrificed their blood for Germany – for a country that had never really given them a chance. We were not meant to suspect that the leading classes of Imperial Germany had made serious mistakes, and that these had jeopardised the victory (if victory had ever been a possibility) as much as the trend on the left had. We were brought up for a world that no longer existed, and we took up nationalistic slogans, while the Republic of which we were trying to make fun was trying to pull the waggon out of the mud.

After graduation, many of our class joined the 'black army'. It was at this point that I, a student and a student apprentice in Stuttgart, broke through this form and saw how wrong we were. Thus, at eighteen, I became immune to the allurements of Hitlerism and could observe the rise of the Weimar Republic with keen interest.

Fritz Ernst **(11)**, pp. 47–8.

document 11
The murder of Walther Rathenau

Although the Freikorps formations set up in Germany in the immediate postwar years were soon officially dissolved, many of them continued to lead a semi-legal existence. In the following extract, the celebrated German author, Ernst von Salomon, who was a Freikorps member, recalls his part in the preliminaries to the murder of the German Foreign Minister, Walther Rathenau (see p. 54).

I think there are two things which it's important not to confuse. First of all there was the plan, the concept that inspired the deed – and then there were the personal motives that induced the individuals to take part in it. The plan itself, how did that arise? Actually there was only one political common denominator that held the whole 'national movement' together at that time, and it was a negative one: it amounted to this: 'We must make an end to *Erfüllungspolitik,* to the policy of accepting the Versailles Treaty and co-operating with the West.' That was the one point on which all the groups and sub-groups were agreed, though they might and did argue about everything else. We had no wish to become a political party with mass support and all that that implies. We did not wish to use the devil to drive out Beelzebub. But we did, from the very beginning, desire basic change, a 'national revolution' that would free us from the material and ideological supremacy of the West as the French revolution had freed France from its monarchy. So our means had to be different from those of the political parties. I think it was Kern himself – it agreed with his logical temperament – who finally said, during a heated argument, that in that case the only course open was to 'eliminate' every *Erfüllungs* politician. To eliminate in that context is, of course, to kill. What other means were there at our disposal? None of those who were repelled by Kern's conclusions could think of any. And once a group was in existence, a very small group, which was so far in agreement, the rest followed more or less automatically, as it were. The atmosphere in which we proposed to carry out a series of assassinations was not unlike that in which the Russian revolutionary Socialists planned theirs – except for the great difference that their deeds were based on belief in a well thought out political and economic doctrine whereas ours were the product of an emotion. Well, the theories of the Revolutionary Socialists have been only very partially fulfilled. There, as here, subsequent developments were almost automatic. There, as here, 'lists' were drawn up. And on one of our lists, among many others, was Rathenau's name.

'That list!' I said. It was, in fact, a single dirty sheet of paper with names scribbled all over it in pencil, some crossed out, some written in again. Many of the names meant absolutely nothing to me, and I had to take quite a lot of trouble

90

to find out who the people were. Incidentally, Theodor Wolff was on the list. I remember thinking that there were a lot of Jewish names. One name, Wassermann, I crossed out myself because I thought it meant Jacob Wassermann, the writer: in fact it was Oskar Wassermann, the banker, a man of whom I knew nothing. The whole thing was drawn up in a fantastically casual way. I didn't set eyes on it until very much later on, in Berlin, when we were in the midst of our preparations for assassinating Rathenau. Kern had left it lying on a table in the boarding house on the Schiffbauerdamm, which was where we were staying at the time. It was pure chance that I took part in the murder of Rathenau; it happened quite 'automatically', because I had become so attached to Kern.

From *The answers of Ernst von Salomon to the 131 questions in the Allied military government 'Fragebogen'*, Putnam, 1954, pp. 55–6.

document 12

The character of the NSDAP

Whilst attempting to become a mass movement, the NSDAP remained essentially a conspiratorial group, as is revealed by the sharp distinction made in the following extract between mere supporters and active members of the party organisation (see p. 46).

When a movement harbours the purpose of tearing down a world and building another in its place, complete clarity must reign in the ranks of its own leadership with regard to the following principles.

Every movement will first have to sift the human material it wins into two large groups: supporters and members.

The function of propaganda is to attract supporters, the function of organisation to win members.

A supporter of a movement is one who declares himself to be in agreement with its aims, a member is one who fights for them.

The supporter is made amenable to the movement by propaganda. The member is induced by the organisation to participate personally in the recruiting of new supporters, from whom in turn members can be developed.

Since being a supporter requires only a passive recognition of an idea, while membership demands active advocacy and defence, to ten supporters there will at most be one or two members.

Being a supporter is rooted only in understanding, membership in the courage personally to advocate and disseminate what has been understood.

Understanding in its passive form corresponds to the majority of mankind which is lazy and cowardly. Membership requires an activistic frame of mind and thus corresponds only to the minority of men.

Propaganda will consequently have to see that an idea wins supporters, while the organisation must take the greatest care only to make the most valuable elements among the supporters into members. Propaganda does not, therefore, need to rack its brains with regard to the importance of every individual instructed by it, with regard to his ability, capacity and understanding, or character, while the organisation must carefully gather from the mass of these elements those which really make possible the victory of the moment.

Adolf Hitler, *Mein Kampf* (118), pp. 520–30.

document 13
Hitler's appeal

In his speeches Hitler came back repeatedly to key themes, finding convenient scapegoats on which to focus public resentment in the distress of postwar Germany. More often than not it was the 'Jew' or 'bolshevik' who was, according to Hitler, the root of Germany's problems. By contrast, the Hitler movement was portrayed as struggling ceaselessly to cut through the jungle of pernicious influences in order to reconstruct a new Germany. The details mattered little; what was important was to convey an exciting sense of purpose about the National Socialists (see p. 45).

Certainly a government needs power, it needs strength. It must, I might almost say, with brutal ruthlessness press through the ideas which it has recognised to be right, trusting to the actual authority of its strength in the State. But even with the most ruthless brutality it can ultimately prevail only if what it seeks to restore does truly correspond to the welfare of the whole people.

That the so-called enlightened absolutism of a Frederick the Great was possible depended solely on the fact that, though this man could undoubtedly have decided 'arbitrarily' the destiny − for good or ill − of his so-called 'subjects', he did not do so, but made his decisions influenced and supported by one thought alone, the welfare of his Prussian people. It was this fact only that led the people to tolerate willingly, nay joyfully, the dictatorship of the great king.

And the Right has further completely forgotten that democracy is fundamentally not German: it is Jewish. It has completely forgotten that this Jewish democracy with its majority decisions has always been without exception only a means towards the destruction of any existing Aryan leadership. The Right does not understand that directly every small question of profit or loss is regularly put before so-called 'public opinion' he who knows how most skilfully to make this 'public opinion' serve his own interests becomes forthwith master in the State. And that can be achieved by the man who can lie most artfully, most infamously: and in the last resort he is not the German, he is, in Schopenhauer's words, 'the great master in the art of lying' − the Jew.

And finally it has been forgotten that the condition which must precede every act is the will and the courage to speak the truth − and that we do not see today − either in the Right or in the Left.

There are only two possibilities in Germany: do not imagine that the people will for ever go with the middle party, the party of compromises: one day it will turn to those who have most consistently foretold the coming ruin and have sought to dissociate themselves from it. And that party is either the Left: and then God help us! for it will lead us to complete destruction − to Bolshevism, or else it is a party of the Right which at the last, when the people are in utter despair, when it has lost all its spirit and has no longer any faith in anything, is determined for its part ruthlessly to seize the reins of power − that is the beginning of resistance of which I spoke a few minutes ago. Here, too, there can be no compromise . . . and there are only two possibilities: either victory of the Aryan or annihilation of the Aryan and the victory of the Jew.

It is from the recognition of this fact, from recognising it, I would say, in utter, dead earnestness, that there resulted the formation of our Movement.

Speech of 12 April 1922, in *Hitler's Speeches* (119), 1, 13–14.

documents 14a, b

The Army in politics

The decision of the German military leaders to put themselves at Ebert's disposal to crush bolshevism saved their own skins and enabled them to carry over into the new Republic much of the spirit and structure of the old German army. This step did not mean that the new army, the Reichswehr, was any the less opposed to the Republic, but what mattered was to build up a united, disciplined force and to eliminate outside influences as far as possible. The abortive attempt to seize power, made by Wolfgang Kapp in 1920, provided Seeckt, the new head of the Reichswehr, with an opportunity to underline the inherent dangers to the Reichswehr's position if it became involved in fratricidal conflicts (see p. 52).

[a] The Field Marshal and I intend to support Ebert, whom I estimate as a straightforward, honest and decent character, as long as possible so that the cart does not slide further to the left. But where is the courage of the middle class? That a tiny minority could simply overthrow the whole German Empire together with its member states, is one of the saddest events of the whole history of the German nation. During four years the German people stood unbroken against a world of enemies – now it permits a handful of sailors to knock it down as if it were a dummy . . .

Groener's letter to his wife on 17 November 1918, cited in Carsten (138), p. 12.

[b] There are numerous indications that many members of the Reichswehr do not see clearly into what a situation we have got through the events of March (Kapp Putsch), and that we must take the consequences for the results of our political short-sightedness. . . . Although it cannot be denied that the majority of misdemeanours can to some extent be

excused on grounds of military obedience, we must nevertheless realise and acknowledge that offences have been committed in our ranks which call for punishment. If we do not admit this ourselves and do not set out on the path of reformation, we must not complain if attempts are made from outside to effect changes. By such offences I not only understand those connected with the political events of the past weeks, but above all the cases of gross indiscipline and brutal behaviour which have occurred in certain units. I do not intend to tolerate or to forget such occurrences. For troops that have tarnished the honour of the soldier there is no room in the Reichswehr . . . We must use all our efforts to eliminate political activity of any kind from the army . . . We do not ask what political opinion the individual has; but I must expect from everybody who continues to serve in the Reichswehr that he takes his oath seriously and has, voluntarily and as an honest soldier, taken his stand on the basis of the constitution . . .

Decree of Seeckt of 18 April 1920, in Carsten **(138)**, pp. 94–5.

document 15
Seeckt's Ostpolitik

Many influential Germans and government officials in the Weimar Republic shared Seeckt's vision of Germany being helped to full recovery through the help of Russia (see doc. 6). Yet Seeckt's insistence on the primacy of German-Russian relations was at variance with the more realistic policy pursued by German foreign ministers after 1919, and in particular by Stresemann, who sought to preserve Germany's revisionist claims against Poland by working with both the East and the West (see p. 31).

Poland's existence is intolerable, incompatible with the survival of Germany. It must disappear, and it will disappear through its own internal weakness and through Russia – with our assistance. For Russia Poland is even more intolerable than for us; no Russian can allow Poland to exist. With Poland falls one of the strongest pillars of the Treaty of Versailles, the preponderance of France. . . . Poland can never offer any advantage to Germany, either economically, because it is incapable of any development, or politically, because it is France's vassal. The re-establishment of the broad common frontier between Russia and Germany is the precondition for the regaining of strength of both countries. 'Russia and Germany within the frontiers of 1914!' should be the basis of reaching an understanding between the two. . . .

We aim at two things: first, a strengthening of Russia in the economic and political, thus also in the military field, and so indirectly a strengthening of ourselves, by strengthening a possible ally of the future; we further desire, at first cautiously and experimentally, a direct strengthening of ourselves, by helping to create in Russia an armaments industry which in case of need will serve us. . . .

In all these enterprises, which to a large extent are only beginning, the participation and even the official knowledge of the German government must be entirely excluded. The details of the negotiations must remain in the hands of the military authorities. . . .

Memorandum by Seeckt, 11 September 1922, in Carsten **(138)**, pp. 140–1.

document 16

Brüning on personalities

As Hermann Müller's 'Great Coalition' struggled without success to tackle the mounting economic and political crisis in Germany after 1928, the Reichswehr leaders began to prepare the ground for the emergence of a new government, which would be based on the more moderate rightist groups in Germany, in order to forestall further successes by the extreme rightist elements. An ideal candidate to head the proposed government, which would be equipped with emergency powers, was Heinrich Brüning, of the Centre Party. The following account gives a revealing and disturbing insight into the system of government in the last years of the Weimar Republic.

A few days later Treviranus came to visit me and said that it was time things were made clear; Groener wanted to discuss the political situation with me. I gave him to understand that all these exchanges were premature and that things could hold out with Hermann Müller until the autumn of 1930. In any case, on grounds of loyalty alone, I could not be the successor of Herman Müller. I would be quite ready to make this clear myself to Groener. . . . I was told that we should meet together on the second evening of Christmas at the Willisens. On this evening, to my astonishment, there were at the Willisens not only Groener and Treviranus but also Schleicher, State Secretary Meissner and Ministerial Director Brandenburg. After the meal, Schleicher and Meissner began to make it clear to me that the Reich President was in no way inclined to leave in office the Müller Cabinet once the Young Plan was settled and that he expected me not to ignore his pleas.

I set out the reasons why I believed that the Müller Cabinet must remain in office under all circumstances until late autumn. Meissner countered by explaining that I would not succeed in convincing the President of my view. Hermann Müller would be toppled and his successor would get powers under Article 48 in the event of emergency. I made the same representations as I had eight months earlier to Schleicher and pointed out that in the summer of 1929 a talk had taken place on my initiative between Hugenberg and Kaas with the purpose of establishing Hugenberg's readiness to form a government with the Centre in the autumn of 1930 in the event of the collapse of the Müller Cabinet.

Hugenberg expressed his agreement, yet one must consider that it would be very difficult for Hugenberg to enter a government immediately after the acceptance of the Young Plan. Quite apart from the fact that the French would surely make difficulties for such a cabinet over the evacuation of the Rhineland. In any case, I considered it politically wrong to deprive Hermann Müller of the fruits of the acceptance of the Young Plan, namely the evacuation of the Rhineland, and burden him only with unpleasant things. That would cause later on an exceptional bitterness, the Left would create an uproar against the vital and far reaching financial and social reforms that were needed, with the result that, as in 1925 and 1927, a cabinet of the Right would again collapse and parliament would again come under the sway of a social democracy that had been once more estranged from *Realpolitik.*

Groener, Schleicher and Meissner replied by stating that there was no question of an appointment for Hugenberg, even in the autumn, the President did not want this man. Consequently, one had to prepare in any case for a difficult situation, which the President foresaw yet did not want to shirk. Groener made admiring remarks about the character and decision of the President which, coming from him, were especially significant for me.

I said that I would never avoid an unpleasant duty, if I had no desire in the normal course of events to be a minister. I had to reaffirm at the same time that the earliest suitable moment for a change of government could only be after the Rhineland evacuation. The mood became cool. I could see that Brandenburg above all was put out by my comments. Groener, Meissner and Willisen remained seated with me. Frau von Willisen went with Schleicher and Treviranus into the next room. There Schleicher told Treviranus: 'So, you see, Brüning won't do it so there's nothing else but for me to do it.'

Groener tried to make it plain to me that he had decisive influence over the old Gentleman (Hindenburg) and that he knew that the President would stand behind me to the last. He asked me to think over the matter again and to go out with him alone one Sunday to talk things over calmly. I expressed my readiness to do this but could not change my opinion.

Brüning's account of the talk, in his *Memoiren 1918–1934*, Stuttgart, Deutsche Verlags-Anstalt, 1970, pp. 150–2.

document 17

Stresemann's speech to the Executive Committee of the DVP, 26 February 1928

Stresemann's career in the Weimar Republic was devoted not only to the conduct of foreign relations but to the development of responsible parliamentary traditions in Germany. Both activities required a constant and exhausting expenditure of energy on Stresemann's part to convince his colleagues in the DVP of the validity of his views (see p. 22).

Let us not fool ourselves about this: we are in the midst of a parliamentary crisis that is already more than a crisis of conscience. This crisis has two roots: one the caricature that has become of the parliamentary system in Germany, secondly the completely false position of parliament in relation to its responsibility to the nation.

What does 'parliamentary system' mean? It means the responsibility of the Reich minister to parliament, which can pass a vote of no confidence and force him to resign. In no way does it entail the allocation of ministerial offices according to the strength of the parliamentary parties. In no way does it entail the transference of government from the cabinet to the parliamentary parties. The minister is designated by the Reich President. It is clear that the President must take into account that ministers named by him secure the support of the majority of the Reichstag. Moreover, the appointment and dismissal of ministers is a question of their personal responsibility. I personally guard against the adoption of the idea that a parliamentary party 'withdraws' its minister. The ministers have to ask themselves whether they will accept office or give it up. The Reichstag can withdraw its confidence from them. The parliamentary party can exclude them from its membership but 'withdrawing' a minister means in reality that the individual ceases to exist and becomes a mere agent of one or another organisation. This conception means the end of liberalism in general. When we no longer have any liberal parties who can put up with the individual then they will cease to be bearers of liberalism.

H. Michaelis *et al.*, eds.,*Ursachen und Folgen. Vom deutschen Zusammenbruch 1918 und 1945 bis zur staatlichen Neuordnung Deutschlands in der Gegenwart,* Berlin, Dokumentation-Verlag, 1958, vol. 7, pp. 236–7.

document 18

Müller's talk with party leaders, 11 December 1929

*Throughout the Republic's history, laborious discussions were needed to secure working agreement between the different parties proposing to form a coalition. Not only did this 'horse-trading' bring the parliamentary process into general disrepect (see **doc. 17**), but it also threatened* *to paralyse governments during periods of crisis. The following passage graphically illustrates the difficulties of the Müller government in tackling the economic crisis in Germany after 1928 (see p. 62).*

Present: Müller, Curtius, Hilferding, Moldenhauer, Wissell, v. Guerard, Schätzel, Stegerwald, Dietrich, Wirth; StS Pünder, Popitz, Trendelenburg; MinDir von Hagenow, Schwerin, v. Krosigk, Zarden, Zechlin; *from the parties:* for the SPD: Breitscheid, Wels, Dittman, Hertz; *for the Centre:* Brüning, Ersing; *for the DVP:* Zapf, Hoff; *for the DDP:* Haas, Fischer; *for the BVP:* Leicht, Horlacher.

(Finance Programme)

The Reich Chancellor called upon the party spokesmen to make known the views of the parties on the government's financial programme.

Deputy *Breitscheid* replied that the discussions of his party were not yet finished. He could, however, already say that his party would indeed participate in the emergency measures but that a commitment to the fourteen individual points of the financial programme did not seem possible. The Social Democracy urgently wanted a crisis to be avoided; they were thus prepared to support the government in the further working out of the financial programme.

Deputy *Zapf* declared that his party could not yet decide to promise their support to the government for the financial programme in its present form. The party strongly distrusted the division of the whole project into immediate measures and a final programme. To agree to the emergency measures without binding guarantees of the final programme being carried out was an impossibility for his party.

Deputy *Brüning* declared that his party could declare itself broadly in agreement with the financial programme, providing the other government parties gave it their approval.

Deputy *Haas* said that the discussions of his party were not yet finished. He hoped, however, that it would be possible to at least come to an agreement on specific points after further debate.

Deputy *Leicht* said that his party completely supported the emergency measures, that they were also ready to give the government a vote of confidence for the foreign policy negotiations at the Hague Conference, but that it was impossible for them to agree to the fourteen points of the whole programme.

The Reich Chancellor concluded on the basis of these remarks that as yet he had not succeeded in getting the parties behind the government. The Reich government nonetheless held firm to its programme and still demanded its complete acceptance by the parties.

Since the further discussion produced no more agreement on the disputed issues, the Reich Chancellor declared that the Cabinet would come to a decision over the situation which had been created by the stand of the parties. He left the party leaders in no doubt, however, that in all probability the decision of the government would be to put the finance programme before the Reichstag, in spite of the negative stand of the parties, in order to achieve a decision in open pitched battle.

Das Kabinett Müller II, Akten der Reichskanzlei, Weimarer Republik, Boppard am Rhein, Harald Boldt Verlag, 1970, vol. 2, pp. 1246–7.

document 19

The elections of summer 1932

The following passage brings out the growing mood of despair amongst responsible commentators on the political scene of Germany after the fall of Heinrich Brüning in 1930. The depressing conclusions were drawn after a long run of success at the polls by the NSDAP.

Looked at politically, objectively, the result of the election is so fearful because it seems clear that the present election will be the last normal Reichstag election for a long time to come. The so-called race of thinkers and poets is hurrying with flags flying towards dictatorship and thus towards a period that will be filled with severe revolutionary disturbances. The elected Reichstag is totally incapable of functioning, even if the Centre goes in with the National Socialists, which it will do without hesitation if it seems in the interests of the party. Genuine bourgeois parties no longer exist. The bourgeoisie has excluded itself as a factor in the political process and will probably have to pay dearly for it.

The one consolation could be the recognition that the National Socialists have passed their peak, since, in comparison with the Prussian elections, they have declined in most constituencies, but against this stands the fact that the radicalism of the right has unleased a strong radicalism on the left. The communists have made gains almost everywhere and thus internal political disturbances have become exceptionally bitter. If things are faced squarely and soberly the situation is such that more than half the German people have declared themselves against the present state, but have not said what sort of state they would accept. Thus any organic development is for the moment impossible. As the lesser of many evils to be feared, I think, would be the open assumption of dictatorship by the present government. . . .

Extract from a memorandum by Reich Minister of the Interior Dr. Külz . in H. Michaelis *et al.,* eds., *Ursachen und Folgen,* vii, 324—5.

Bibliography

Any reader familiar with the history of the Weimar Republic will recognise at once the debt owed to books in the German language. The requirements of the series preclude listing these at any length. Those few German works which are listed are those to which I have directly referred in the main text.

GENERAL ACCOUNTS

1 Angell, J. W., *The Recovery of Germany,* Yale University Press, 1929.

2 Bracher, K. D., *Die Auflösung der Weimarer Republik. Eine Studie zum Problem des Machtverfalls in der Demokratie,* 4th edn., Schwarzwald, Ring-Verlag, 1964.

3 Cambridge University Press, 1960. *A Short History of Germany 1815–1945.*

4 Carr, William, *A History of Germany 1815–1945,* Edward Arnold, London, 1969.

5 Castellan, G., *L'Allemagne de Weimar 1918–1933,* Paris, Libraire Armand Colin, 1969.

6 Chickering, R. P., 'The Reichsbanner and the Weimar Republic 1924–1926', *Journal of Modern History,* xl, no. 4, 1968, 524–34.

7 Craig, G. A., 'Engagement and neutrality in Weimar Germany' *Journal of Contemporary History,* ii, no. 2, 1967, 49–63.

8 Dorpalen, Andreas, *Hindenburg and the Weimar Republic,* Princeton University Press, 1964.

9 Eksteins, M., 'The *Frankfurter Zeitung*: Mirror of Weimar democracy', *Journal of Contemporary History,* vi, no. 4, 1971, 3–28.

10 Epstein, K., *Matthias Erzberger and the Dilemma of German Democracy,* Princeton University Press, 1959.

11 Ernst, Fritz, *The Germans and Their Modern History,* Columbia University Press, 1966.

12 Eyck, E., *A History of the Weimar Republic,* 2 vols, paperback edn, J. Wiley, 1967.

13 Feuchtwanger, E. J., *Prussia: myth and reality,* London, Oswald Wolff, 1970.

14 Flenley, R., *Modern German history*, 4th rev. edn., Dent, 1968.

15 Gay, Peter, *Weimar Culture. The outsider as insider*, Secker & Warburg, 1969.

16 Gooch, G. P., *Germany*, Benn, 1926.

17 Holborn, H., *A History of Modern Germany 1840–1945*, Eyre & Spottiswoode, 1969.

18 Hopwood, R. F., ed., *Germany: people and politics 1750–1945*, Oliver & Boyd, 1968.

19 Jasper, G., ed., *Von Weimar zu Hitler 1930–1933*, Cologne, Berlin, Kiepenheuer & Witsch, 1968.

20 Kohn, Hans, ed., *German History. Some new views*, Allen & Unwin, 1954.

21 Laqueur, W. Z., *Young Germany. A history of the German youth movement*, Routledge, 1962.

22 Lebovics, Herman, *Social Conservatism and the Middle Classes in Germany 1914–1933*, Princeton University Press, 1969.

23 Lewis, B. I., *George Grosz: art and politics in the Weimar Republic*, University of Wisconsin Press, 1971.

24 Liang, Hsi-Huey, *The Berlin Police Force in the Weimar Republic*, University of California Press, 1970.

25 Mann, Golo, *The History of Germany since 1789*, Chatto & Windus, 1968.

26 Meinecke, F., *The German Catastrophe*, Boston, Beacon Press, 1963.

27 Morgan, R., ed., *Germany 1870–1970. A hundred years of turmoil*, London, BBC, 1970.

28 Nicholls, A. J., *Weimar and the Rise of Hitler*, Macmillan, 1968.

29 Nicholls, A. J., and Matthias, E., eds., *German democracy and the triumph of Hitler: Essays in recent German history*, Allen & Unwin, 1971.

30 Niewyk, D. L., *Socialist, Anti-semite, and Jew. German social democracy confronts the problem of anti-semitism 1918–1933*, Louisiana State University Press, 1971.

31 Parker, R. A. C., *Europe 1919–1945*, Weidenfeld & Nicolson, 1969.

32 Ramm, Agatha, *Germany 1789–1919, A political history*, Methuen, 1967.

33 Ringer, Fritz K., *The Decline and Fall of the German Mandarins: the German academic community 1890–1933*, Harvard University Press, 1969.

34 Rodes, J. E., *The Quest for Unity. Modern Germany 1848–1970*, Holt, Rinehart & Winston, 1971.

35 Rosenberg, A., *Imperial Germany. The birth of the German Republic 1871–1918,* paperback reprint, Oxford University Press, 1970.

36 Rosenberg, A., *A History of the German Republic,* Methuen, 1936.

37 Salomon, Ernst von, *The Captive: the story of an unknown political prisoner,* Weidenfeld & Nicolson, 1961.

38 Stern, Fritz, *The Failure of Illiberalism. Essays on the political culture of modern Germany,* Knopf, 1972.

39 Symposium. *The Road to Dictatorship. Germany 1918–1933. A symposium by German historians,* London, Oswald Wolff, 1970.

40 Wheeler-Bennett, J., 'The end of the Weimar Republic. A reconsideration', *Foreign Affairs,* 1, no. 2, 1972, 351–71.

41 Wheeler-Bennett, J., *Hindenburg: The wooden titan,* Macmillan, 1936.

42 Williamson, J. G., *Karl Helfferich 1872–1924,* Princeton University Press, 1972.

43 Zorn, W., 'Student politics in the Weimar Republic', *Journal of Contemporary History,* v, no. 2, 128–43.

CONSTITUTION/REVOLUTION

44 Burdick, C. B., and Lutz, R. H., *The Political Institutions of the German Revolution,* Praeger, 1966.

45 Carsten, F. L., *Revolution in Central Europe 1918–1919,* London, Temple Smith, 1972.

46 Feldman, G. D., *Army, Industry and Labour in Germany 1914–1918,* Princeton University Press, 1966.

47 Hunt, R. N., 'Friedrich Ebert and the German revolution of 1918' in L. Krieger and F. Stern, eds., *The Responsibility of Power. Historical essays in honour of H. Holborn,* Macmillan, 1968, pp. 315–34.

48 Rürup, R., Problems of the German revolution 1918–1919, *Journal of Contemporary History,* iii, no. 4, 1968, 109–35.

49 Ryder, A. J., *The German Revolution of 1918. A study of German socialism in war and revolt,* Cambridge University Press, 1967.

50 Toynbee, A., ed., *The Impact of the Russian Revolution 1917–1967,* Oxford University Press, 1967.

51 Tracey, D. R., 'Reform in the early Weimar Republic: the Thuringian example', *Journal of Modern History,* xliv, no. 2, 1972, 195–212.

52 Bretton, H. L., *Stresemann and the Revision of Versailles*, Stanford University Press, 1953.

53 Cobban, A., *The Nation State and National Self-determination*, Collins, Fontana, rev. edn., 1969.

54 Cornebise, A. A., 'Gustav Stresemann and the Ruhr Occupation: the making of a statesman', *European Studies Review*, ii, no. 1, 1972, 43–67.

55 Craig, G. A., *From Bismarck to Adenauer. Aspects of German statecraft*, Harper Torchbooks, 1965.

56 Darmstaedter, F., *Germany and Europe. Political tendencies from Frederick the Great to Hitler*, Methuen, 1945.

57 Dehio, L., *Germany and World Politics in the Twentieth Century*, Chatto & Windus, 1959.

58 Dyck, H. L., *Weimar Germany and Soviet Russia 1926–1933. A study in diplomatic instability*, Chatto & Windus, 1966.

59 Freund, G., *Unholy alliance*, Chatto & Windus, 1957.

60 Gasiorowski, Z. J., 'The Russian overture to Germany of December 1924', *Journal of Modern History*, xxx, 1958.

61 Gasiorowski, Z. J., 'Stresemann and Poland before Locarno', *Journal of Central European Affairs*, xviii, 1958, 25–47.

62 Gasiorowski, Z. J., 'Stresemann and Poland after Locarno', *Ibid*, 292–317.

63 Gatske, Hans W., 'Gustav Stresemann: A bibliographical article', *Journal of Modern History*, xxvi, March 1964, 1–13.

64 Gatske, H. W., *Stresemann and the Rearmament of Germany*, Johns Hopkins Press, 1954.

65 Hilger, G. and Meyer, A. G., *The Incompatible Allies*, New York, Macmillan, 1953.

66 Holborn, H., 'Diplomats and diplomacy in the early Weimar Republic', in G. Craig and F. Gilbert, eds., *The Diplomats*, paperback reprint, Atheneum Press, 1968, vol. i.

67 Jacobson, J., *Locarno Diplomacy*, Princeton University Press, 1972.

68 Kimmich, C. M., *The Free City. Danzig and German Foreign policy 1918–1934*, Yale University Press, 1968.

69 King, J. C., *Foch versus Clemenceau: France and German disarmament 1918–1919*, Harvard University Press, 1960.

70 Kochan, L., *Russia and the Weimar Republic*, Cambridge, Bowes & Bowes, 1954.

71 Kollman, E. C., 'Walther Rathenau and German foreign policy. Thoughts and actions', *Journal of Modern History*, xxiv, 1952, 127–42.

72 Korbel, J., *Poland between East and West. Soviet and German diplomacy towards Poland 1919–1933*, Princeton University Press, 1963.

73 Laqueur, W., *Russia and Germany. A century of conflict*, Weidenfeld & Nicolson, 1965.

74 Luckau, A., *The German delegation at the Paris Peace Conference*, Columbia University Press, 1941.

75 Mayer, A. J., *Politics and Diplomacy of Peacemaking. Containment and counter-revolution at Versailles 1918–1919*, Weidenfeld & Nicolson, 1968.

76 Nelson, H. I., *Land and Power. British and Allied policy on Germany's frontiers 1916–1919*, Routledge & Kegan Paul, 1963.

77 Newman, W. J., *The Balance of Power in the Interwar Years 1919–1939*, Random House, 1968.

78 Riekhof, Harald von, *German-Polish relations 1918–1933*, Johns Hopkins Press, 1971.

79 Robertson, E., ed., *The Origins of the Second World War*, Macmillan, Student edition, London, 1971.

80 Schulz, G., *Revolution and Peace Treaties 1917–1920*, Methuen, 1972.

81 Taylor, A. J. P., *The Origins of the Second World War*, rev. edn., Hamish Hamilton, 1963.

82 Watson, D. R., 'The making of the Treaty of Versailles', in N. Waites, ed., *Troubled Neighbours. Franco-British relations in the twentieth century*, Weidenfeld and Nicolson, 1971.

PARTIES/COALITION POLITICS

83 Berlau, A. J., *The German Social Democratic Party 1914–1921*, New York, 1949.

84 Burnham, W. D., 'Political immunization and political confessionalism: the United States and Weimar Germany', *Journal of Interdisciplinary History*, iii, no. 1, 1972, 1–30.

85 Heberle, R., *From Democracy to Nazism. A regional case study on political parties in Germany*, Baton Rouge, 1945.

86 Hunt, R. N., *German Social Democracy 1918–1933*, Yale University Press, 1964.

87 Laubach, E., *Die Politik der Kabinette Wirth 1921–1922*, Lübeck & Hamburg, Matthiesen Verlag, 1968.

88 Morsey, R., *Die deutsche Zentrumspartei 1917–1923*, Düsseldorf, Droste Verlag, 1966.

89 Neumann, S., 'Germany: changing patterns and lasting problems', in Neumann, ed., *Modern political parties: Approaches to comparative politics*, University of Chicago Press, 1957, 354–90.

90 Neumann, S., *Die Parteien der Weimarer Republik*, paperback reprint, Stuttgart, W. Kohlhammer Verlag, 1965.

91 Turner, H. A., *Stresemann and the Politics of the Weimar Republic*, Princeton University Press, 1963.

92 Zeender, J. K., 'The German Catholics in the Presidential election of 1925', *Journal of Modern History*, xxv, no. 4, 1963, 366–81.

ECONOMICS/REPARATIONS

93 Bennett, E. W., *Germany and the diplomacy of the financial crisis*, Harvard University Press, 1962.

94 Bergmann, C., *The History of Reparations*, Boston, 1927.

95 Bry, G., *Wages in Germany 1871–1945*, Princeton University Press, 1960.

96 Felix, D., *Walther Rathenau and the Weimar Republic. The politics of reparations*, Johns Hopkins Press, 1971.

97 Keynes, J. M., *The Economic Consequences of the Peace*, Macmillan, 1920.

98 Ringer, F. K., *The German Inflation of 1923*, Oxford University Press, 1969.

99 Stolper, Gustav, *The German Economy 1870 to the Present*, Weidenfeld & Nicolson, 1967.

LEFTIST OPPOSITION

100 Angress, W. T., *Stillborn Revolution. The Communist bid for power in Germany*, Princeton University Press, 1963.

101 Comfort, R. A., *Revolutionary Hamburg Labour Politics in the early Weimar Republic*, Stanford University Press, 1966.

102 Mitchell, A., *Revolution in Bavaria 1918–1919. The Eisner Regime and the Soviet Republic*, Princeton University Press, 1965.

103 Nettl, J. P., *Rosa Luxemburg*, 2 volumes, Oxford University Press, 1966.

104 Waldman, E., *The Spartacist Uprising of 1919*, Maquette University Press, 1958.

105 'The bolshevization of the German Communist party', *The Times Literary Supplement*, 25 June 1970, 685–6.

RIGHTIST OPPOSITION

106 Allen, W. S., *The Nazi Seizure of Power: the experience of a single German town, 1930–1935*, Eyre & Spottiswoode, 1966.

107   Braatz, W. E., 'Two Neo-Conservative myths in Germany 1919–1932', *Journal of the History of Ideas,* Oct.–Dec. 1971, 569–84.

108   Bracher, K. D., *The German Dictatorship. The origins, structure and effects of National Socialism,* Praeger, 1970.

109   Broszat, M., *Der Staat Hitlers. Grundlegung und Entwicklung seiner inneren Verfassung,* Deutscher Taschenbuch Verlag, Bd 9, 2nd ed., Munich, 1971.

110   Bullock, A., *Hitler – A study in tyranny,* Odhams Press, 1960.

111   Butler, R. D'O., *The Roots of National Socialism 1783–1933,* reprint, New York, Howard Fertig, 1968.

112   Carsten, F. L., *The Rise of Fascism,* Batsford, 1967.

113   Chanady, A., 'The disintegration of the German National People's Party, 1924–1930', *Journal of Modern History,* xxxix, 1967, 65–91.

114   Cohn, N., *Warrant for Genocide: the myth of the Jewish world conspiracy and the protocols of the Elders of Zion,* Eyre & Spotiswoode, 1967.

115   Edmondson, N., 'The Fichte society. A chapter in Germany's conservative revolution', *Journal of Modern History,* xxxviii, 1966, 161–80.

116   Fest, J. C., *The Face of the Third Reich,* Penguin Books (Pelican), 1972.

117   Hertzmann, L., *DNVP-Right-wing Opposition in the Weimar Republic,* Nebraska University Press, 1963.

118   Hitler, A., *Mein Kampf,* transl. R. Mannheim, Hutchinson, 1969.

119   Hitler, A., *The Speeches of Adolf Hitler April 1922 to August 1939,* ed. N. H. Baynes, 2 vols, Oxford University Press, 1942.

120   Jarman, T. L., *The Rise and Fall of Nazi Germany,* Signet Books, New York, 1961.

121   Klemperer, Klemens von, *Germany's New Conservatism, its history and dilemma in the twentieth century,* Princeton University Press, 1957.

122   Maser, W., *Hitler's 'Mein Kampf': an analysis,* trans. R. H. Barry, Faber, 1970.

123   Mosse, G. L., *The Crisis of German Ideology. Intellectual origins of the Third Reich,* Weidenfeld & Nicolson, 1966.

124   Mosse, G. L., 'The genesis of fascism', *Journal of Contemporary History,* i, no. 1, 1966, 14–26.

125   Noakes, J., *The Nazi Party in Lower Saxony 1921–1933,* Oxford University Press, 1971.

126   Nolte, E., *Three Faces of Fascism,* Weidenfeld & Nicolson, 1965.

127 Orlow, D. O., 'The organizational history and structure of the NSDAP 1919–1923', *Journal of Modern History,* xxxvii, no. 2, 208–26.

128 Orlow, D. O., *A History of the Nazi Party 1919–1933,* vol. 1, David and Charles, 1971.

129 Phelps, R. H., 'Before Hitler came, Thule Society and Germanen Orden', *Journal of Modern History,* 1963, no. 3, 245–61.

130 Pulzer, P. G. S., *The Rise of Political Anti-semitism in Germany and Austria,* Wiley, 1964.

131 Schoenbaum, D., *Hitler's social revolution. Class and status in Nazi Germany 1933–1939,* Weidenfeld & Nicolson, 1967.

132 Schramm, P. E., *Hitler: the man and military leader,* Penguin Press, London, 1972.

133 Stern, H., 'The organization consul', *Journal of Modern History,* xxxv, 1963, 20–32.

134 Turner, H. A. Jnr, 'Hitler's secret pamphlet for industrialists 1927', *Journal of Modern History,* xl, no. 3, 1968, 348–74.

135 Waite, R. G. L., *Vanguard of Nazism. The Free Corps Movement in postwar Germany 1918–1923,* Harvard University Press, 1952.

136 Woolf, S. J., *European Fascism,* Weidenfeld & Nicolson, 1968.

137 Zeman, Z. A. B., Nazi Propaganda, Oxford University Press, 1964.

REICHSWEHR

138 Carsten, F. L., *The Reichswehr and Politics 1918–1933,* Oxford University Press, 1966.

139 Craig, G. A., *The Politics of the Prussian Army 1640–1945,* Oxford University Press, 1955.

140 Demeter, Karl, *The German Officer Corps in Society and State 1650–1945,* Weidenfeld & Nicolson, 1965.

141 Goerlitz, Walter, *History of the German General Staff 1657–1945,* Praeger, 1967.

142 Gatske, H., 'Russo-German military collaboration during the Weimar Republic', *American Historical Review,* lxiii, 1957–8, 565–97.

143 Gordon, H. J., *The Reichswehr and the German Republic 1919–1926,* Princeton University Press, 1957.

144 Hallgarten, G. W. F., 'General Hans von Seeckt and Russia 1920–1922', *Journal of Modern History,* xxi, 1949, 28–34.

145 Seeckt, H. W., *Thoughts of a Soldier,* London, 1930.

146 Seeckt, H. W., *The Future of the German Empire,* London, 1930.

147 Wheeler-Bennett, J. W., *Nemesis of power. The German army in politics 1918–1945,* Macmillan, 1961.

Index